REPRODUCTIVE
RIGHTS

Who Decides?

VICKI ORANSKY WITTENSTEIN

TWENTY-FIRST CENTURY BOOKS / MINNEAPOLIS

To Lily, Tommy, and Eve, and to future generations of parents
everywhere. And as always, for Andy, who makes everything
possible and wonderful.

Acknowledgments: Many thanks to Stephanie Toti, senior counsel, Center for
Reproductive Rights, and Willie Parker, MD, for standing on the front lines in the
fight for reproductive rights. I also want to thank Helen M. Alvaré, professor of
family law, George Mason University School of Law, for her scholarly voice in the
pro-life movement. I greatly appreciate my sister-in-law, Kate Wittenstein, professor
of history and gender, women and sexuality studies at Gustavus Adolphus College,
who offered invaluable assistance and source information.

 This book would not be possible without my wonderful editor, Domenica
Di Piazza, who encouraged me to tackle this difficult subject and whose dazzling
editorial skills contributed so much to the book. Brianne Johnson at Writer's House
enthusiastically supported me and was a valuable sounding board on this project.

 Thanks also to Andy, Ted, Alyssa, Amanda, Jeff, and Mom; my dear family and
friends; and my colleague Diana Childress, who always cheer me on.

Twenty-First Century Books
A division of Lerner Publishing Group, Inc.
241 First Avenue North
Minneapolis, MN 55401 USA

For reading levels and more information, look up this title at www.lernerbooks.com.

Main body text set in Garth Graphic Std 11.5/16.
Typeface provided by Adobe Systems.

Library of Congress Cataloging-in-Publication Data

Wittenstein, Vicki O., 1954–
    Reproductive rights : who decides? / Vicki Oransky Wittenstein.
      pages cm
    Includes bibliographical references and index.
    ISBN 978-1-4677-4187-3 (lb : alk. paper) — ISBN 978-1-4677-8804-5 (eb pdf)
    1. Reproductive rights—History—Juvenile literature. 2. Birth control—History—
Juvenile literature. 3. Family planning—History—Juvenile literature. I. Title.
    HQ766.W57 2016
    363.9'609—dc23   2014040830

Manufactured in the United States of America
1 – VP – 12/31/15

TABLE OF CONTENTS

THE FIGHT FOR REPRODUCTIVE FREEDOM

In the twenty-first century, it's hard to imagine what family life would be like without an understanding of human reproduction, access to contraception, and high-quality medical care. Yet around the globe, hundreds of thousands of women die yearly in childbirth and from lack of prenatal care, particularly in developing (poor) countries. While prenatal care is available in all clinics in the United States, many women cannot afford the care and go without it. Additionally, access to birth control and sex education in the United States is not a guaranteed right, although it is in some nations.

Through the course of history, millions of women endured failing health and even death from multiple pregnancies and childbirths. Birth control was unreliable, and millions of women also suffered serious injury and death from unsafe abortions.

Because of these perils, without knowledge of medicine and science, women looked for ways to avoid pregnancy. In ancient societies, for example, some women wore pouches containing cat livers (which were thought to have magical qualities) on their left feet. Some women inserted objects soaked in donkey's milk into their vaginas to avoid conceiving. In more recent centuries, many men wore condoms (materials that cover the penis) made from linen or animal intestines during sex as a form of contraception and to avoid sexually transmitted disease (STD). By the mid-nineteenth

In the twenty-first century, reproductive health includes a wide range of devices, technologies, and procedures for birth control and conception. Access to and use of reproductive health care typically depends on religious and community beliefs as well as income levels.

century, manufacturing processes had increased the strength of rubber and more men across all social classes began to use rubber condoms.

But by the late nineteenth century, talking publicly about sex and reproductive health was illegal in the United States. Courageous activists such as Margaret Sanger and Mary Ware Dennett were arrested for writing about these subjects. In the next century, the development of the birth control pill in 1960 was a medical and historical milestone that allowed women to control pregnancy and direct the course of their own lives.

In the United States of the twenty-first century, reproductive health is hotly debated. For example, assisted reproductive technologies (ART) for infertile couples raise new ethical and moral issues about sex selection, surrogacy (an agreement to create a pregnancy for intended parents), and the disposal of human embryos (fertilized eggs). Sex education is also controversial. Many states do not mandate sex

Condom History

For thousands of years, men wore condoms to guard against sexually transmitted diseases. In ancient Egypt, men fashioned protective sheaths from goat membranes, and in 1563, Italian anatomist Gabriel Fallopius invented a linen sheath during an epidemic of syphilis, a type of STD. Scanty evidence exists as to when sheaths were first used for contraception. But in a letter written in 1671 Madame de Sévigné, a French aristocrat, advised her daughter to avoid pregnancy by using goldbeater's skins (named for a process that used animal membranes to beat gold into thin, pliable sheets of gold). By the early nineteenth century, American men were using condoms fashioned from animal intestines and even silk for contraception.

In 1839 Massachusetts-based inventor Charles Goodyear patented the vulcanization of rubber, a heating process that made rubber stronger and flexible and led to the widespread manufacture of condoms. At this time, condoms were also called French male safes, capotes, goldbeater's skins, and gentleman's protectors. Inventors also created a host of rubber birth control devices for women. Called pessaries (objects inserted into the vagina, uterus, or cervix), they included womb veils (diaphragms and cervical caps) and intrauterine devices (IUDs). Many women liked pessaries because they could use them secretly, as a backup in case condoms or other methods failed.

education in public schools. In some of the states that do offer sex education, information must stress only abstinence (refraining from sex). Birth control is generally available to minors without parental consent but to varying degrees, depending on the state.

Almost all insurance plans cover prescription drugs, but some states do not require companies to pay for all contraception approved by the US Food and Drug Administration (FDA). Some states permit pharmacists to refuse to fill prescriptions for contraception or to dispense emergency contraception if doing so conflicts with the provider's religious or moral beliefs. In a 2014 case, *Burwell v. Hobby Lobby Stores, Inc.,* the US Supreme Court weighed in as well. The court ruled that family-owned businesses whose owners claimed religious objections could refuse to provide insurance coverage for certain types of birth control to their employees.

ABORTION

In the United States, abortion has been one of the most contentious flash points in the area of women's reproductive rights. It is a moral, political, and legal issue that has divided families and friends and has sometimes led to violent confrontations. Over the course of US history, abortion has been outlawed at different times and in different states. But in a landmark decision in 1973—*Roe v. Wade*—the US Supreme Court ruled that women have a fundamental right to abortion guaranteed by the US Constitution.

In the decades since that ruling, though, state laws and lower court rulings have limited funding to clinics that provide abortions. Many states have enacted laws designed to persuade women not to have abortions. States have also mandated that small abortion clinics comply with the strict regulations required by outpatient surgical centers. In combination, these restrictions have led to clinic closures, leaving women in some states with few places, if any, to obtain legal abortions. In other rulings, courts have limited the types of abortions that are available to women. For example, some late-term abortions that were legal at the beginning of the 1990s are no longer legal in the twenty-first century.

Human Reproductive Systems

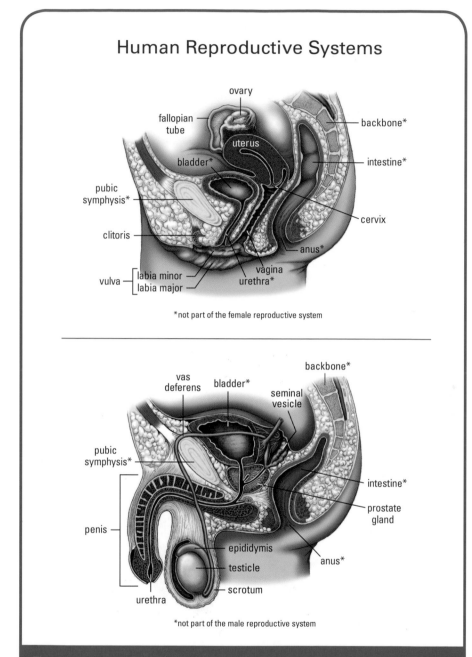

The top diagram illustrates the anatomy of the female reproductive system, while the bottom diagram shows the anatomy of the male reproductive system. Conception typically occurs through sexual intercourse between a male and a female, although a range of reproductive technologies allow infertile, single, and LGBT couples to have children as well.

GOING BY THE NUMBERS

Since 2008 US abortion rates, as well as rates of adolescent pregnancy and childbirth, have reached historic lows. The Guttmacher Institute, an organization based in New York City and Washington, DC, conducts global research on sexual and reproductive health and seeks to protect and expand reproductive rights worldwide. The Guttmacher studies show that from 2008 to 2011, abortion rates in almost all states dramatically declined to 16.9 abortions per 1,000 women (ages 15 to 44), the lowest rate since 1973. Still, the rate of abortion in the United States remains high. According to the institute, "By age 45, about half of American women will have an unintended pregnancy, and nearly 1 in 3 will have an abortion."

Arguments on both sides are passionate, and many people are neither entirely pro-choice nor entirely pro-life. Many pro-choice Americans have moral qualms about having an abortion themselves but recognize that family members and friends may need one. Many pro-life people support abortion in cases of rape or incest or when a mother's health is at risk.

But even when politics, culture, and religion have frowned upon contraception and abortion or deemed them illegal, women and medical practitioners have always found ways to share information about reproduction, to delay childbirth, to space or end pregnancies, and to safeguard reproductive health. As medical historian Norman E. Himes has noted, birth control "fulfills some fundamental human need" that "dates from pre-history." Americans are still debating the implications of this statement in the twenty-first century.

CHAPTER 1
HERBS, MAGIC, AND OTHER EARLY BIRTH CONTROL PRACTICES

Walk three times around a tree where a pregnant wolf has urinated. Dangle a weasel's testicles between your thighs. Drink a potion mixed with the skin of a snake or foam from a camel's mouth. Try pouring the camel foam over your genitals. Drape a magical amulet (lucky charm) containing the bones of a black cat around your neck.

To avoid pregnancy, women in southwestern Asia and Europe turned to these kinds of rituals in centuries past. In ancient Egypt, a recipe in the Kahun Papyrus, written in 1850 BCE, and in the later Ramesseum Papyrus IV of 1784–1622 BCE, recommended that a woman stuff her vagina with "feces of crocodile . . . [and] fermented dough" to avoid becoming pregnant.

Why did ancient Egyptians and other peoples think these techniques would work? Mainly because they knew very little about human reproduction. It wasn't until 1677 that Antonie van Leeuwenhoek, the famed Dutch inventor of microscopes, and his student Johan Ham van Arnhem first identified sperm, calling the swimming cells "animalcules." Another 250 years would pass before scientists began untangling the mysteries of female ovulation (the discharge of eggs from a woman's ovaries) and its relationship to pregnancy. It would not be until the 1920s that scientists in Japan and Austria finally understood the female menstrual cycle.

Until modern science grasped the basics of fertility,

people around the world turned to magic, herbs, medicine men and women, and religion for birth control. By trial and error, people discovered contraception that worked—at least some of the time. For example, modern researchers have shown that the Egyptian crocodile dung recipe, as well as an elephant dung recipe favored by ancient Indians, may have actually prevented conception. The dung and the fermented dough contained properties that, like some modern methods of birth control, may have changed the chemical balance in the vagina. In the altered environment, sperm would die. In general, pessaries may have been effective because they blocked access to the opening of the cervix, through which sperm must swim to get to a woman's egg.

Ancient people also created myths to explain the mysteries of reproduction and contraception. Some early humans thought that certain fruits contained a child's spirit and that eating them would lead to pregnancy. Others believed that

This illustration from the Ebers Papyrus (1550–1500 BCE) depicts a woman giving birth *(left)*, aided by maids and a midwife. Ancient Egyptians had a wealth of recipes and methods to promote reproductive techniques, including birthing, abortion, and contraception. Some of them worked, while others did not.

weather conditions and the powers of the sun or the moon were responsible for pregnancy. Women were warned about bathing in water, as some cultures believed that eels, snakes, and other fish might cause pregnancy. In the twenty-first century, we might joke about storks carrying new babies into the world. But ancient peoples from many cultures revered the ibis, a relative of the stork, as a bearer of children. For example, the ancient Teutons of northern Europe thought that storks collected the souls of children from swamps and delivered them to families wanting babies. The belief was so strong that if a woman who didn't want a baby saw a stork, she would drive the bird away.

THE ANCIENT WORLD

Women and men living in different regions of the world and during different time periods relied on similar birth control methods, many of which are still used in the modern era. For example, over the centuries, people abstained from sex; avoided sexual intercourse at certain times during a woman's menstrual cycle; inserted pessaries to block and kill sperm; ingested oral preparations; and practiced prolonged breast-feeding, which can delay ovulation for many months and thus prevent pregnancy. Men used condoms and practiced coitus interruptus (withdrawing the penis from the vagina before ejaculation). Throughout history, more extreme measures to deal with unwanted pregnancy have included abortion and infanticide (the killing of newborns).

The world's earliest humans did not read or write, so ideas about reproduction and birth control were passed down orally from ancestors. Many of the methods were unreliable and could cause serious infections. For example, Bapinda and Bambunda women in central Africa contracted vaginal infections from stuffing their vaginas with rags or grass to space their pregnancies apart. Australian, Polynesian, and Melanesian girls drank potions containing spider eggs, snakeskins, herbs, and roots. The mixtures were thought to create magic that would prevent pregnancy. Similarly, Canelo tribal women in South America drank a medicine containing the crushed roots of a plant said to have mystical powers and prevent conception. After sex, they ate only birds and unsalted roasted plantains. According to tradition, a woman had to follow this ritual very carefully to avoid pregnancy. In North America, Cherokee women swallowed a root called spotted cowbane for four days in a row if they wanted to become sterile forever.

The ancient Egyptians took a scientific approach based on an early understanding of chemistry. In the Ebers Papyrus (1550–1500 BCE), Egyptian scholars recorded recipes for both contraception and abortion, which modern researchers think may actually have worked. One recipe advised women to "moisten a pessary of plant fiber" containing "[u]nripe fruit of acacia, Colocynth, Dates . . . [and] 6/7 pint of honey" and to insert it into the vagina. Researchers have discovered that when the leaves of an acacia plant undergo fermentation, lactic acid is produced. Lactic acid repels and kills sperm and is an ingredient in many twenty-first-century spermicides.

In the Berlin Papyrus (ca. 1300 BCE), the ancient Egyptians recorded the first written documentation of an oral contraceptive. The text tells a woman to first "fumigate her vagina with emmer seeds to prevent her receiving the semen . . . [next prepare] a prescription to loosen semen [containing] oil, celery, sweet beer . . . [then] heat and drink for four mornings."

Ancient Greek and Roman scholars prescribed different remedies for contraception and abortion. To abort a pregnancy, women drank a brew of water, wine, vinegar, or honey, and plants such as rue, myrtle, and myrrh. Greek and Roman women ate pine, pomegranate, pennyroyal, and artemisia for contraception.

The ancient Greek philosopher Aristotle advocated population control as a way to build and maintain an "ideal city." In the fourth century BCE, he wrote that "if conception occurs in excess of the limit so fixed, . . . have abortion induced before sense and life have begun in the embryo." As for methods of contraception, Aristotle wrote in *Historia Animalium* (ca. 350 BCE) about "anoint[ing] that part of the womb on which the seed falls with oil of cedar, or with ointment of lead or with frankincense, comingled with olive oil." As is true with many modern-day spermicides, Aristotle's oil mixture probably slowed the sperm on the way to their target, making conception less likely.

In *Diseases of Women*, Hippocrates, a Greek doctor also writing in the fourth century BCE, advised that a woman should drink "[diluted] copper ore. . . . For a year, thereabouts, she does not get pregnant." Contemporary researchers have not studied the effects of swallowing copper for birth control. But they have found a benefit to using copper intrauterine devices, which release trace amounts of copper that aid in killing sperm.

Contraceptive practices eventually spread from ancient Greece and Rome to the Islamic world, in the ancient Middle East. Physicians in tenth-century Persia (in Iran) such as al-Razi, Ali-ibn al-Abbas, and Ali ibn Sina (also known as Avicenna) considered contraception to be part of good medical care. To prevent pregnancy, they prescribed pessaries to block the cervix or, when soaked in a variety of crushed herbs and fruit juices, to kill sperm. In addition to recommending coitus interruptus and pessaries, physicians suggested coating the penis with substances such as rock salt, tar, juice of an onion, or oils that would function as barriers and slow down or kill ejaculated sperm. Ibn Sina recommended that after intercourse, women jump backward "seven or nine times" and try to "provoke sneezing," which would supposedly force sperm out of the vagina.

THE CHAIN OF LEARNING WEAKENS

During medieval times, or the Middle Ages (ca. 500–1500 CE), European physicians knew about contraceptive and abortion techniques and even invented new ones. However, the Roman Catholic Church dominated European social and political life during the Middle Ages. The church counseled celibacy (abstention from sex) for its priests and sexual restraint for its followers. The church, along with new laws, limited reproductive practices. For example, a law enacted by King Edward I of England (who reigned from 1272 to 1307) proclaimed, "He who oppresses a pregnant woman . . . so as to cause an abortion, or who give to her [something] that she will not conceive . . . is guilty of homicide." In other words, both contraception and abortion were illegal.

The Renaissance, which began in the late Middle Ages in Italy and spread through Europe into the seventeenth century, was a period of rediscovery of, interest in, and expansion of the learning of the ancient Greeks and Romans. But Renaissance physicians had few new ideas about birth control—at least none that were recorded. Most likely the church's position against birth control had an effect on limiting advancements in contraception and abortion.

In addition, the universities where physicians trained focused on medical theory instead of working directly with

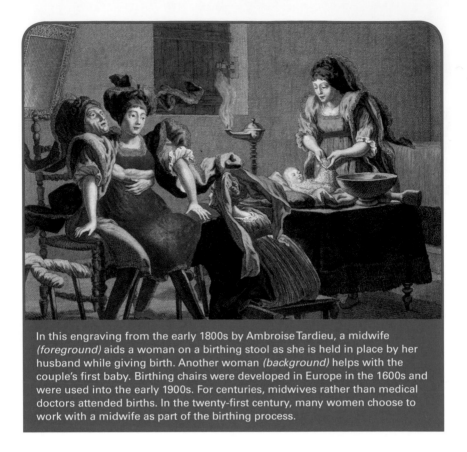

In this engraving from the early 1800s by Ambroise Tardieu, a midwife *(foreground)* aids a woman on a birthing stool as she is held in place by her husband while giving birth. Another woman *(background)* helps with the couple's first baby. Birthing chairs were developed in Europe in the 1600s and were used into the early 1900s. For centuries, midwives rather than medical doctors attended births. In the twenty-first century, many women choose to work with a midwife as part of the birthing process.

patients. While doctors had historically dealt with childbirth and birth control, the midwives of Renaissance Europe— typically older women trained through experience rather than at universities—were increasingly more responsible for delivering babies and attending to women's reproductive health. Arriving when expectant mothers first started labor, midwives encouraged the entire family to be present in the birthing room to support the mother. Midwives knew how to stitch vaginal wounds and how to tie the umbilical cord. They also helped new mothers with breast-feeding. Since they no longer attended to pregnant women, physicians of this era did not learn about childbirth or the benefits of folk medicine.

COLONIAL AMERICA

The English settlers who arrived in North America in the early to mid-seventeenth century were mostly staunch Puritans or members of other Protestant denominations that observed strict religious beliefs. In what they viewed as the New World, colonial couples needed many children to help farm the land, care for animals, and assist with household chores. Protestant colonists also wanted to build large and successful communities based on strict morals, so they hoped to increase, rather than decrease, their numbers. The colonists believed that God wanted them to "be fruitful and multiply," a directive written in the Bible. Many women saw reproduction as "their natural calling" although, as a woman named Mary Clap wrote, "bearing, tending and Burying children was Hard work." For these reasons, colonists barely whispered about contraception, if they talked about it at all. As a result, by the end of the seventeenth century, the population of English colonists in North America began to double with each generation.

Stillbirths, miscarriages, and infants dying during birth or shortly thereafter were common in colonial America because of a lack of medical knowledge about prenatal care, childbirth, and infant care. Infant death rates were so high (nearly 25 percent in some areas) that most women gave birth—without anesthetics to dull the pain—to about eight children in the hopes that three to seven might live into adulthood. Many young people died from childhood diseases that would not be eradicated until the twentieth century. Mary Clap died at the age of twenty-four after giving birth to six children and burying four of them.

When colonial Americans did try to control the spacing of their children and the size of their families, they most often

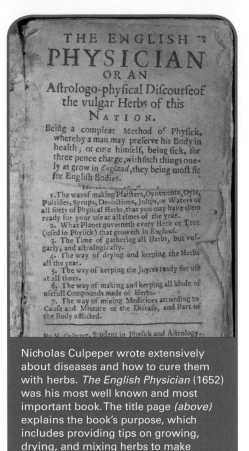

Nicholas Culpeper wrote extensively about diseases and how to cure them with herbs. *The English Physician* (1652) was his most well known and most important book. The title page *(above)* explains the book's purpose, which includes providing tips on growing, drying, and mixing herbs to make ointments, syrups, and other treatments for disease.

engaged in coitus interruptus, prolonged breastfeeding, and abortion. The English colonials brought knowledge of these techniques from across the ocean and were familiar with the popular herbs and plants used for abortion in Europe. Although books were scarce in colonial America, many colonials read Nicholas Culpeper's *The English Physician* (1652) and the *Complete Herbal* (1653), which suggested botanical remedies for "female complaints" a polite way of referring to pregnancy, childbirth, and abortion. American Indians and slaves from Africa and the Caribbean also taught white colonial women about herbs that induced abortions. But most often, colonial women quietly picked up information from relatives or close friends or discovered abortion recipes folded into family Bibles, letters, or cookbooks.

By the end of the eighteenth century, wives and husbands complained in diaries and letters about the dangers to a woman's health of birthing so many children. Although few statistical studies exist on the frequency of death in childbirth in colonial America, most people knew women who had died while delivering a baby. Women called childbirth the "Dreaded [operation]" and "that [evil] hour I [look] forward to with dread." Many women faced serious gynecological problems after childbirth, problems that they endured for the rest of their lives and that worsened with repeated pregnancies.

THE AMERICAN REVOLUTION

The American Revolution (1775–1783) liberated American society from British rule, and the United States was born. The war transformed the role of women. In white colonial America before the war, men were the heads of the household. They watched over the finances, made decisions about raising the children, and expected women to run the household smoothly. Husbands viewed their wives as subordinates and dependents. When men went off to war to battle the British, women stepped in to manage the finances and the land. When the men returned, they found wives, sisters, and other female relatives who no longer viewed themselves as inferior to men and who began to push for more equality.

By the end of the eighteenth century, the view that God and nature controlled reproduction had begun to change. Women began to enlist men as partners in limiting the number of children, and historians point to a marked reduction of fertility by the end of the century. One study of Quaker families in Delaware, New Jersey, New York, and Pennsylvania found that about 40 percent of Quaker women marrying before 1770 gave birth to nine or more children. After 1770 only about 14 percent of married women had as many births. And among those who married after 1790, 12 percent bore no children—a significant drop in family size. At the turn of the century, the early Victorian era would usher in new ideas about reproduction, sexual morality, and family planning.

CHAPTER 2
BIRTH CONTROL IN THE VICTORIAN AGE

Attitudes toward sex and reproductive health changed dramatically during the Victorian era, which was named after England's famous queen, Victoria, who reigned from 1837 to 1901. According to social standards, the ideal Victorian white woman was "delicate, refined, and chaste." Middle- and upper-class white women did not work outside the home. They depended on their husbands, fathers, or brothers to financially support them. Even in working-class families, where women were more likely to hold jobs, men remained the heads of household and the decision makers. Without economic independence and meaningful jobs, most women relied on marriage and motherhood for a sense of worth. They were not expected to take control of their reproductive lives but to follow church doctrine and let God dictate when they had children.

Black women of the era lived with different types of challenges. More likely than white women to work for a living, black women faced rampant racism. In 1865 Congress passed the Thirteenth Amendment to the US Constitution, abolishing slavery. As freed individuals, black women and their families looked for new ways to support themselves. Black women in rural areas worked as sharecroppers (farmers who pay rent to work a small plot of someone else's land). In the cities, they were more likely to find work as maids in white people's homes or as laundresses. They too felt the pressure to bear children as a mark of respectable womanhood.

In many world cultures, the stork (or its relative the ibis) has been a symbol of the bearer of children for centuries. In this Victorian-era postcard, a genteel lady fends off a stork in the hopes of avoiding pregnancy.

These notions about the ideal Victorian woman spilled over into sexual relations within marriage. In the nineteenth-century, laws proclaimed that a woman had a duty to have sex with her husband and could not legally refuse sexual relations with him. State laws defined rape as occurring between a man and a single woman and exempted husbands from charges of forcible sex with their wives. (In fact, rape within marriage was not a crime until the 1970s, when US states began to repeal the marital exemptions.)

Yet despite these well-defined roles for women, new ideas about sexuality and reproduction began to challenge social constraints. Advertisements for condoms, female preparations to induce abortion, and contraceptive devices such as ladies' protectors and womb veils began to appear in newspapers and periodicals, sporting and racing magazines, and home medical manuals. Congregationalist minister and writer John Todd observed a new commercial trend in the late 1860s.

He noted that provocative ads were arriving in the mail of young women in New England shortly after they announced their marriages in local newspapers. The ads provided all that was needed "by which the laws of heaven in regard to the increase of the human family may be thwarted [stopped]." Contraception, abortion, and sexual intimacy, once only spoken about in hushed terms in private, were permeating public discourse, mostly among men. What had happened?

GOING PUBLIC

In the early to mid nineteenth century, American society changed rapidly. Young men and women left family farms to take jobs in the nation's new factories and shops in growing cities. The size of families began to shrink, as parents living in cities no longer needed children to work farmland. Urbanization intensified social problems such as poverty, delinquency, alcoholism, and prostitution. But city life also offered easier access to knowledge. Advice literature, newspapers, pamphlets, and novels abounded about the social and political issues of the day, including sexual and reproductive freedom.

A profusion of literature on reproductive issues slowly created an aura of acceptance for contraception and abortion. In fact, by mid to late century, most married women were practicing some form of birth control, favoring douching, the rhythm method (having sex at those times during the menstrual cycle when ovulation is least likely to occur), and coitus interruptus. The wealth of new information fascinated Americans, even as it frightened them. They were shaken by the religious and moral implications of controlling pregnancy and by the idea of separating sex from reproduction. In this era of new freedoms and more open discussion of sex and reproduction, many Americans worried about a moral domino effect. Would the public airing of information about birth control and its availability lead to sexual promiscuity and sex outside of marriage? Would sexual promiscuity break apart the family and leave women without financial support? Would God condemn people for engaging in sex without procreation as the goal?

Although Americans expressed shock at explicit descriptions of sexual matters, they nonetheless used the information to learn about sex without the embarrassment of speaking to others. For example, many Americans read Robert Dale Owen's and Charles Knowlton's informative documents, written in plain English, about sexuality, reproduction, and contraception. In *Moral Physiology; or A Brief and Plain Treatise on the Population Question* (1831), social reformer Owen argued that contraception was necessary for population control and to protect the world's food supply. Owen's close friend Frances Wright influenced his thinking. A well-known radical social reformer, Wright had fled to Europe to escape the shame of having become pregnant as a single woman. Owen was one of the only writers during the nineteenth century to consider the contraceptive needs of single women. He wrote that men needed to practice sexual restraint. Failing that, Owen advocated coitus interruptus, vaginal sponges, and condoms. His book was so popular that thirteen editions were published in thirty years.

Personal experience also greatly influenced Knowlton, a Boston physician. He observed the hardships his wife endured by giving birth to four children over the course of eight years. In a frank discussion of reproductive control in the *Fruits of Philosophy* (1832), Knowlton argued that contraception was as natural as getting a haircut or trimming a man's beard.

In this humorous 1872 engraving, men blow up condoms to check for holes. Condoms are one of the oldest forms of contraception in the world.

Knowlton believed contraception required female participation. He advised women to douche with spermicides, a method he claimed to have invented. (It had actually been in use since ancient times.) His detailed lists of chemical substances popularized douching across the United States. He also was the first in the nation to graphically write about the female genitals so that readers would understand how to put his contraceptive "checks" to use. In later editions of his book, he discussed sperm, male sexual organs, and conception. Although much of Knowlton's knowledge about reproduction was inaccurate, his explanations did give readers enough information to promote his birth control methods.

In his lecture travels around the United States, Knowlton noted that even among those who were interested in his book, "[they] won't speak out for it in public—they are too afraid." At the time, Vermont, Connecticut, and Massachusetts had laws against publishing and selling books that were considered obscene. Knowlton's book was in this category. In fact, Knowlton stood trial four times between 1832 and 1835 for violating Massachusetts obscenity laws. In one trial in 1832, he was fined fifty dollars, even though the jurors sympathized with him. As one of the jurors told him afterward, "I like your book and you must let me have one of them." But Knowlton was not always so lucky. After a conviction in 1833, he spent three months in jail enduring forced hard labor.

For women of the early nineteenth century, public discussion of sexual practices and reproductive health was improper and unthinkable. Without the right to vote and without power to make political change, women who spoke out were ridiculed. By mid-century, though, social reformer and feminist Mary Gove Nichols began to break through the silence. She and her husband opened a bookstore in New York City to sell their writings about reproductive control. Historians think that Nichols and her husband jointly wrote a book called *Esoteric Anthropology* (1853), even though he is the only named author. Sections in the book express daring views for the time. One passage says, "If a woman has any right in this world it is the right to herself; and if there is anything in this world she has a right to decide, it is who shall be the father of her children. She has an equal right to decide whether she will have children and to choose the timing for having them."

Racier titles such as *A Confidential Letter to the Married* and *The Wife's Secret of Power* lured readers in the mid-nineteenth century. Many small pamphlets written under pseudonyms or by unnamed authors dealt with pregnancy and abortion. But unlike the earlier works of Owen and Knowlton, these documents were thinly veiled advertisements for contraception and abortion products.

Most writers at this time encouraged contraception only to protect a woman's health. In the nineteenth century, many women still suffered a lifetime of ill health from consecutive pregnancies spaced too closely together. Thousands also died from lack of prenatal care, during childbirth, from puerperal fever (infections of the female reproductive organs after childbirth), and from unsafe abortions. In *The Physical Life of Woman* (1872), physician and women's medical adviser George Napheys wrote, "There is definitely such a thing as *over-production*—having too many children." Napheys quoted a Dr. Tilt, who had earlier written that too many pregnancies also produced unhealthy and "puny children." To serve as good mothers and wives, Napheys urged women to practice reproductive control.

ON THE LECTURE CIRCUIT

At about this time, Americans were flocking to public lectures for educational purposes as well as for entertainment. Reformers lectured to people in rural and urban settings across the country, speaking about marriage and motherhood, women's rights, slavery and the abolition (antislavery) movement, and the dangers of alcohol. Some even hinted at support for contraception. As time went by, lectures on reproduction became more explicit. Lecturers taught about anatomy and reproduction and even offered sexual advice. The qualifications of the lecturers and the style of the talks varied greatly. Initially, many lecturers gave sensationalistic talks. In later years, they were more tactful and dignified. Many physicians were highly critical of lectures about the human body, which they felt were unsuitable for decent society.

Lecturer Mary Gove Nichols attracted large audiences of women, first in Boston as a lecturer for the Ladies' Physiological Society, then in other cities of New England as well as in Philadelphia and New York. Many found her lectures about reproductive issues shocking and embarrassing. In later years, she lectured to mixed audiences of men and women, but mostly she arranged for small groups of women to meet to discuss intimate female health issues, menstruation, and contraception.

Men and women living in towns and cities east of the Mississippi River clamored to hear self-proclaimed physician Frederick Hollick speak about anatomy, conception, prenatal care, and sexual desire. He was so popular that from 1845 until 1850, he conducted twenty-six lectures in Philadelphia and spoke in Washington, DC, before former US president John Quincy Adams and members of Congress. He even lectured on board a steamship traveling to New Orleans, Louisiana. By 1852 Hollick had authored eleven books about sexuality, marriage, and general health.

With a delivery style that respected people's sensitivity to sexual matters, he contributed to the growing acceptance of public discussion of reproduction. Using the removable parts of papier-mâché and wax models of the human body, he demonstrated the reproductive systems. In advertisements for his lectures, Hollick claimed, "Many have even *fainted away* at a first view [of the models], from the impression that they were viewing a real body." This likely was his way of promising exciting entertainment that would still be appropriate for proper women.

Recognizing a need for greater knowledge about reproductive control, in 1847 Hollick was one of the first to lecture on the benefits of the rhythm method. The method operated on the principle that women couldn't conceive during certain times in the menstrual cycle. Hollick's initial advice that women abstain from sexual intercourse for at least fifteen days after menstruation may have been somewhat helpful. But his later recommendation that women need wait only six or eight days after menstruation was unsound, as that is the most fertile period for many women.

Slavery: Reproduction without Freedom

In 1861, when Rose Williams, an African American slave in Texas, was just sixteen years old, her master forced her to live with another slave named Rufus. At first, Rose thought she was supposed to keep house for Rufus. But one night, he crept into her bed and tried to rape her. She defended herself with a fire poker. The next day, as Rose later recounted, her master explained the consequences of continuing to refuse Rufus's sexual advances: whipping at the stake.

If you were a teenage slave like Rose, a white master owned you. You could not decide when or whether to become pregnant, and your children were born slaves. Slave owners wanted slave women to give birth to as many children as possible, to increase the number of slaves who worked the master's plantation. Masters bought and sold slave women like they would a plow horse, and a woman's value was measured by the number of babies she was capable of producing. As one planter reported, "A breeding woman is worth from one-sixth to one-fourth more than one who does not breed."

The law did not recognize marriage as a legal contract between slaves or between a female slave and a white man. Rape of a slave was not considered a crime. Masters frequently forced sexual mating between slaves they thought of as "prime stock," regardless of whether the slaves were in relationships with other partners. Masters and plantation overseers also routinely raped and sexually abused female slaves at will. The end result for slave women was repeated pregnancy.

In the South, slave women who worked the fields endured extreme physical labor as they planted and picked crops in hot and humid weather. Slave mothers had to work during pregnancy and immediately after childbirth. They carried their newborns with them while they worked the fields. In 1850 more than twice as many black infants died as white infants and fewer than two out of three lived until the age of ten. Many deaths were due to poor nutrition. Slave children were also harmed by the auctioning of slave women to plantation owners for profit. Auctions typically split up families and separated mother and child, usually forever.

Abortions and miscarriages were far more common among slave

Oh my child my child.

Mothers with young Children at work in the field.

While they were working in plantation fields, slave mothers either strapped their babies on their backs *(left)* or left them on the side of the field *(right)* where they were exposed to insects and other animals. This woodcut illustration, depicting the cruelty of an overseer—appeared in the *Anti-Slavery Almanac* in 1840. The mission of the monthly publication was to educate and persuade readers of the evils of slavery and of discrimination against people of color.

women than white women. Dr. John T. Morgan from Tennessee wrote in 1860 about the ways slaves tried to control reproduction, including by "violent exercise" and "external and internal manipulation." Midwives sometimes secretly aided women who wanted an abortion. The women also aborted by drinking brews and inserting pessaries containing herbal ingredients, such as pennyroyal, rue, and the "roots and seed, of the cotton plant." Some desperate slave women killed their newborns.

But many slave women fought back and resisted unwanted sexual advances, even if it meant suffering through whippings or other physical punishments. Some pretended to be ill or ran away to avoid sex. One former slave recounted the story of a Virginia kitchen slave named Sukie Abott, who repelled her master's advances while she was making soap by "pushing him, rear end first, into a pot of boiling lye. He got up holdin' his hindparts an' ran from de kitchen."

PURITY AND VOLUNTARY MOTHERHOOD

After the 1850s, Americans grew increasingly uncomfortable with the commercialization of contraception and abortion and of the idea of women's reproductive control. Many reacted by forming various groups to restore "social purity" in society. Some reformers, feeling that commercialization led to the depravity of young men, argued for restricting the sex trade. Feminists, though, were more focused on restricting male sexual behavior and on expanding women's reproductive rights.

By the 1870s, three groups of feminists were arguing for voluntary motherhood, or the right of a woman to decide for herself if she wanted to bear children. A woman's right to abstain from sex was the central idea of voluntary motherhood. Nineteenth-century laws, however, stated that women must submit sexually to their husbands. Feminists regarded these laws as violating a woman's sense of personhood.

Among the three leading feminist groups were suffragists, who fought for the rights of women to own property, become educated, and vote in elections. The suffragists included women such as Elizabeth Cady Stanton and Susan B. Anthony. A second group, including social purists such as Elizabeth Blackwell, Ida Craddock, and the Woman's Christian Temperance Union, organized against prostitution, drunkenness, and other behavior that they considered to be immoral. Victoria Woodhull and members of "free-love" groups were against traditional marriages. Free lovers felt that marriage laws kept unhappy spouses together, turned couples into bad parents, and constrained love.

In the nineteenth century, feminist groups did not equate contraception with greater sexual freedom, as women do in the twenty-first century. Instead, they promoted motherhood as a woman's most important role in life—one that gave women a sense of identity and ensured economic support through marriage. They opposed artificial devices or methods of contraception, which took some of the threat of pregnancy away from sex, and therefore, according to some feminists, promoted promiscuity and extramarital affairs. If a couple decided to mutually abstain from sex, feminists preferred natural methods, such as a male remaining celibate for a period of time or refraining from ejaculation during sex. Men as well as women spoke out about voluntary motherhood. From the late 1840s into the 1860s, Presbyterian minister Henry

Victoria Woodhull *(above, in the 1890s)* fought for workers' rights, women's rights, and civil rights for freed slaves. She was the first woman to attempt to run for president of the United States. In 1872 she was chosen as the presidential candidate for the Equal Rights Party. However, she was a controversial personality because of her radical views and was arrested on obscenity charges, spending Election Day in jail. In the end, her name did not actually appear on the ballot.

Clarke Wright, an advocate for sexual reforms in marriage, lectured in New England, New York, and Pennsylvania about responsible parenting and "the unwelcome child." Women, he believed, had the absolute right to abstain from sex. After all, they were the ones who would endure pregnancy and the ultimate responsibility for a child. His urgent pleas to couples and unmarried women for "designed [planned] maternity" conveyed his belief in birth control. Women, he advised, should not marry men who refused to talk before marriage about the spacing of the children they might have together.

He counseled: "Wives! be frank and true to your husbands on the subject of maternity and the [sexual] relation that leads to it. Interchange thoughts and feelings with them."

Birth control methods at this time were very unreliable, and many women who used them became pregnant anyway. For this reason, feminists such as Elizabeth Cady Stanton and Victoria Woodhull refused to condemn women for having abortions, although they did not approve of the procedure. They viewed abortion as cruel punishment for women who were the victims of men's sexual desires.

The legality of abortion in the United States at this time varied by decade and by state. Women desperate to end unwanted pregnancies who lived in places or times in which abortion was illegal often tried to induce abortion on their own. To do so, they would drink poison or insert sharp, often unsterile objects, such as knitting needles, into the uterus. Many women died as a result. Feminists, though, did not advocate legalized abortion as a solution to these problems. By improving education for girls and women, winning women the right to vote, and advancing equality and sexual respect between the sexes, feminists hoped to promote a society where abortion would no longer be necessary. As the periodical *Woman's Advocate* in Ohio proclaimed: "'Till men learn to check their sensualism, and leave their wives free to choose their periods of maternity, let us hear no more invectives [insulting language] against women for the destruction of prospective [expected] unwelcome children."

But despite the voluntary motherhood movement, which focused on abstinence, thousands of women across the country were swept up in the exploding commercialism of reproductive control. They read about the newest birth control fads, attended lectures, bought new contraceptive products, and induced abortions.

THE ABORTION DEBATE

Ann Trow Lohman, better known as Madame Restell, was the most prominent and outspoken New York City abortionist in the mid to late nineteenth century. A former seamstress, Restell lacked formal medical training. But even so, her services were so popular that she opened additional offices in Boston and Philadelphia. Salesmen traveled door-to-door selling Restell's pills, which promised to induce spontaneous abortions. If the pills didn't work, customers were advised to travel to her New York City office for more invasive abortion procedures. Restell boasted that no one ever died as a result of her services. She seems to have taken good care of her patients and, if necessary, nursed them overnight.

Restell became quite wealthy through her practice. She dressed in expensive silks and furs, rode the streets of New York in a grand horse-drawn carriage, and built a showy townhouse on fashionable Fifth Avenue. Although many saw her as an example of an increasingly immoral and promiscuous society, she did not care.

Restell was not alone in offering abortions at this time. The high numbers of women seeking to end pregnancies supported the businesses of more than two hundred abortionists just in New York City. From 1840 until 1880, a booming business thrived in pills, liquid medicines, and botanic and herbal mixtures to end pregnancy. American women also purchased hooks and other instruments from pharmacists or by mail to perform abortions on their own.

Many abortionists were well trained, but others were quacks. Some promoted risky concoctions and surgeries, and many women died as a result of infection and hemorrhagic (uncontrolled) bleeding. Doctors and others who offered abortion services in the United States did so in a landscape of shifting legal attitudes toward the practice. Before the 1850s, Americans followed the English common law (a body of law inherited from colonial times). Common law permitted abortion before quickening—that is, when a woman could feel the fetus move for the first time, usually late in the fourth month or early in the fifth month of pregnancy. Many women intentionally aborted before quickening, and many did so even afterward.

Abortionists competed against one another to stay in business. Sensationalist trials of slipshod abortionists riveted the nation, and advertisements commercialized the practice. Advertisers used discreet language that women knew were code words for pregnancy and abortion. For example, in the *Boston Daily Times* during the week of January 4, 1845, a Dr. Carswell advertised: "Particular attention given to all Female complaints, such as Suppressions [of menstruation]. . . . Dr. Carswell's method of treating these diseases [pregnancies], is such as to remove the difficulty [by abortion] in a few days. . . . Strict secrecy observed and no pay taken unless a cure is performed." In an 1871 article, the *New York Times* reported that Restell spent approximately $60,000 a year advertising her services—the equivalent of about $1,180,000 in the early twenty-first century.

In mid-century, during one decade alone (1850s), one abortion occurred for every five to six live births. Why did so many American women seek abortions? In earlier decades, desperate single women sought abortions to avoid the stigma of bearing a child out of wedlock. But as attitudes loosened, married women who did not want a child for health, economic, or social reasons also aborted their unwanted pregnancies. This was especially true among middle- and upper-class women, who usually could afford the procedure. It was also the case for Protestant women, since Protestant churches were less outspoken against abortion than the Catholic Church. Social purists pointed to the domino effect of contraception to explain the rise in abortion. They felt that access to contraception led to more sex for pleasure (instead of procreation), which led to more abortions if the contraception failed. Those against women's rights blamed feminists for increased numbers of abortions. They claimed that women had become self-indulgent and cared more about their position in society than raising children. Large numbers of women, on the other hand, embraced the ideas of family limitation and controlling pregnancy.

PHYSICIANS CRUSADE AGAINST ABORTION

In the nineteenth century, very few doctors with formal medical instruction were trained in contraception and abortion. (The American Medical Association, or AMA, did not approve contraception as part of a physician's standard training until the 1930s.) So the vast number of women went to irregular doctors—midwives and abortionists without formal medical training—for these services. If women were pleased with the results, they frequently approached these practitioners for other health issues as well.

Most nineteenth-century physicians in the United States vehemently opposed abortion. Their reasons varied. They worried, in part, about the health risks of abortion. They also resented the growing numbers of irregular doctors who competed with and threatened their businesses.

To rid the profession of untrained competitors, physicians

formed the AMA in 1847. The association aimed to establish trained doctors as the nation's specialists in medicine. By requiring medical licensing to practice, the AMA was able to put the irregular doctors out of business and to ban many dangerous practices and harmful substances. Dr. Horatio Robinson Storer, a Boston-based specialist in gynecology and obstetrics (medical and surgical specialties in female reproductive health, pregnancy, and childbirth), led the AMA's antiabortion crusade. The AMA viewed "true women" as those who accepted their "God-given duty" to reproduce. The organization labeled those women who thought otherwise as unnatural and selfish. The AMA also claimed that women with such views supported deviant behavior that would break up the family.

Storer, like other physicians of the time, was convinced that abortions caused health problems for women such as abdominal aches and pains and weakened bladder control. He also doubted whether quickening was a legitimate cutoff point for abortion. Storer gathered statistics on abortions, miscarriages, and stillbirths from doctors around the country. His research and subsequent report became the basis of the AMA's support for criminalizing abortion in 1859.

Many physicians opposed abortion for political and racist reasons. They saw that as more middle- and upper-class white women had begun to control their own reproduction and to limit the size of their families, the nation's white population was declining. Like many Victorian-era politicians and legislators, physicians feared that free blacks and the large numbers of immigrants entering the country would outpace the American-born white population. Storer captured these fears in his concerns about the growth of new settlements in the American West. "Shall they be filled with our [white,

American-born] children or by those aliens [immigrants]?" he asked. "This is the question that our own [white] women must answer, upon their loins [birthing of children] depends the future destiny of the nation."

The AMA's antiabortion campaign, as well as the efforts of social purists and some feminists, influenced a wave of restrictive state laws criminalizing abortion. As early as 1821, Connecticut had become the first state to criminalize abortions after quickening. Within forty years, most states had similar laws. Usually the physicians, midwives, or apothecaries (pharmacists) who supplied the abortifacients (substances that induce abortion) were punished—not the women themselves. This changed in 1845, when New York began to prosecute women who had abortions. Other states followed New York's example and prosecuted women who aborted. By the end of the 1880s, most states prosecuted abortion providers, regardless of the stage of pregnancy at which the procedure was performed. Convicted of manslaughter or second-degree homicide, abortionists faced jail time.

The new antiabortion laws scared away many doctors from performing the procedure and put nonphysicians out of business. Yet pregnant women with money who were seeking an abortion could find a doctor who would perform the procedure. Even so, the antiabortion climate drove many American women—both well-off and poor—to secret and drastic measures to end unwanted pregnancies.

CHAPTER 3
CONTRACEPTION BANNED

When Anthony Comstock, the son of a wealthy farmer from Connecticut, arrived in New York City in the 1870s, prostitutes wandered the streets hawking their services. They hung pictures of themselves in shop windows and advertised in local newspapers. Saloons hosted dance shows, where female entertainers stripped or provocatively flirted with drunken crowds. In the run-down rooming house where Comstock lived, young men ogled pornographic pictures and magazines. In his ramblings throughout the city, Comstock observed the commercial sex trade: pornography, how-to sex manuals, and contraceptive devices. As one commentator noted, "Hardly a newspaper [exists] that does not contain . . . open and printed advertisements, or a drug store whose shelves are not crowded with nostrums [unreliable contraceptive devices] publicly and unblushingly displayed."

One of Comstock's New York friends confided that he had contracted an STD from a prostitute. Comstock was incensed. Upon discovering that an obscene book had tempted his friend to visit the prostitute, Comstock bought a copy of the book and showed it to the local police captain. Because obscenity had been outlawed in New York City, Comstock and the police captain arrested the book dealer, Charles Conroy. Comstock targeted Conroy in two more arrests between 1868 and 1874. The third arrest so infuriated Conroy that he slashed Comstock in the head.

Like Comstock, Morris Ketchum Jesup and a group of wealthy lawyers and businessmen were social purists. They were horrified by the sex trade as well as by the commercial trade in contraception and abortion. They viewed these public elements of American life as expressions of vice (immorality), which they feared would tempt young men. Jesup and his followers approved of Comstock's campaign and began to fund his anti-vice efforts. In 1873 they established the New York Society for the Suppression of Vice (NYSSV). Comstock was appointed head of the organization. The NYSSV authorized him and other NYSSV agents to help police officers track down purveyors of obscenity. Soon vice organizations sprang up across the country, from Boston to San Francisco. The hunt for sellers of contraceptive items and information had begun.

The antiobscenity Comstock Act of 1873 was named after Anthony Comstock *(above)*, head of the NYSSV. In 1895 an editorial in the *New York Times* coined the term *comstockery,* to refer to censorship of literature and theatrical performances on grounds of immorality. Famous British playwright George Bernard Shaw popularized the term in the early 1900s, when one of his plays— *Mrs. Warren's Profession* (about a former prostitute and her daughter)—became a target of Comstock censorship efforts.

THE COMSTOCK ACT

Comstock was unhappy about the federal government's approach to obscenity. A federal law, passed in 1865, outlawed "[any] obscene book, pamphlet, picture, print, or other publication . . . [of] vulgar and indecent character" sent through the mails. Advertisements, though, were not included. Abortifacients and contraceptives did not make the list of obscene items either. Comstock lobbied the US Congress for a stronger federal law.

In 1873 Congress passed an amendment to the federal obscenity law. Officially called the Act for the Suppression of Trade in, and Circulation of, Obscene Literature and Articles of Immoral Use, the law would come to be known as the Comstock Act, named for the man who worked so hard for its passage.

In one section, the law punished those who sent "obscene, lewd, or lascivious" materials through the mail. For the first time, the prohibited items included "any article or thing designed or intended for the prevention of conception or procuring of abortion." Under the new law, Americans could be convicted of a misdemeanor for mailing obscene items, advertisements for them, or information about where these items could be acquired. Punishment was harsh. Violators could receive from one to ten years of hard labor for each offense and a fine of $100 to $5,000.

The law went beyond restricting materials sent through the mail in Washington, DC, and in US territories. It also punished the possession, sale, lending, exhibiting, advertising, giving away, or publishing of obscene articles, including "any article whatever for the prevention of conception, or for causing unlawful abortion." Violators could be punished with six months to ten years of hard labor or a fine of up to $2,000. This section of the act served as a model for twenty-four states that went on to limit reproductive control by passing similar laws. Some states passed even more restrictive laws, such as penalizing private discussions about contraception or abortion. Eleven states criminalized the simple possession of information about reproductive control. In 1879 Connecticut enacted the strictest law of all, outlawing the use of contraceptive devices and medicines. Connecticut's law remained in place for almost a century, until the US Supreme Court struck it down in 1965.

THE LIMITS OF THE OBSCENITY LAWS

Working as an agent of the US Postal Service, Comstock was the chief enforcer of the Comstock Act. He made more obscenity arrests than anyone else in the United States. But his fiery campaign did not guarantee convictions. Judges were wary of government intrusion into people's lives, and courts were lenient with those who violated the law. NYSSV agents arrested only 105 people for birth control crimes from 1873 to 1898. Of these, 38 percent were not convicted. Only 16 of the 65 people who were convicted served time in jail. Two US presidents, Ulysses S. Grant and Rutherford B. Hayes, together pardoned 6 individuals sentenced to jail on obscenity charges. As historian Andrea Tone noted, Comstock never had the satisfaction of seeing one person sentenced to the maximum punishment under the law that bore his name.

Judges as well as newspapers attacked Comstock's distasteful tactics. The press frequently portrayed Comstock as a laughingstock. Cartoonists drew caricatures emphasizing his big handlebar mustache. One victim of Comstock's methods, which usually involved trickery, was Restell. In 1878, posing as a poor husband with too many mouths to feed, Comstock convinced Restell to sell him an abortifacient for his wife and then arrested Restell. She had been arrested several times before and had already served time in jail. But as a sixty-seven-year-old woman, she could not bear the idea of spending more time behind bars. Journalists reported that

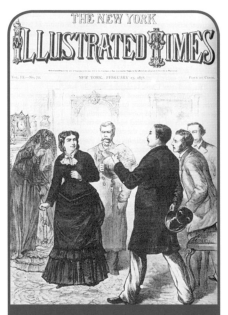

Anthony Comstock's arrest of abortionist Ann Lohman (Madame Restell) made the cover of the February 23, 1878, edition of the *New York Illustrated Times.*

she donned a nightgown covered in diamonds, lay down in a bathtub, and slit her throat.

REPRODUCTIVE CONTROL GOES INTO HIDING

In a letter she wrote in 1885, Rose Williams explained to her recently married friend Alletie Mosher, "You want to know of a sure preventative. . . . They are called Pessairre [pessaries] or female preventative. . . . They cost one dollar. . . . The Directions are with it." Many people like Rose and Alletie wanted birth control devices. Yet because they were outlawed under the Comstock Act, these products and services went underground (were sold illegally). As with abortion, wealthier women had little problem finding what they needed and paying for it, even if the devices and birth control products were illegal.

Fear of jail or of being shamed by the community prevented most people from speaking out against the law. Many books about reproductive control fell out of print, and newer books were less helpful. Inventors seeking patents for new birth control devices carefully avoided any wording that would make it clear that a device would be used for birth control. One Texas inventor, for example, applied for a patent for a "male pouch" that was actually a condom. Sellers

Comstock on the Rampage

In volumes of notebooks, Anthony Comstock neatly recorded the names and addresses of those he arrested, their offenses, the status of each case, and comments. A NYSSV list of "Obscene Matter Confiscated" up until 1890 included the following:

Book and Sheet Stock seized and destroyed . . . 64,723 lbs. [29,358 kilograms]

Obscene Pictures and Photos . . . 872,507

Articles for Immoral Use, of rubber, etc. . . . 97,132

Boxes of Pills, Powders, &c., used by Abortionists . . . 8,502

Circulars, Catalogues, Songs, Poems, etc. . . . 1,598,777

Newspapers containing unlawful Advertisements or Obscene Matter . . . 34,547

who continued to advertise used words such as *protection* and *security*. They avoided saying that a product prevented conception.

The Comstock laws, physicians such as Storer, and other social purists silenced public discussion about sexual intimacy, contraception, and abortion. They left behind a society divided between those who could afford contraception and abortion and those who could not. At the dawn of the twentieth century, women's small gains in reproductive rights and control over their own bodies were stymied.

CHAPTER 4
MARGARET SANGER, BIRTH CONTROL PIONEER

In 1910 Margaret Sanger; her husband, Bill; and their three children moved to New York City. There, Sanger, who was a nurse, began helping poor women deliver babies. Most of the women Sanger nursed lived in crowded and run-down tenements (slums) in Manhattan's Lower East Side, where infectious diseases thrived. Sanger was sympathetic to the women, as her mother had died at the age of forty-nine of tuberculosis (TB), a disease of the lungs. Her mother's TB had worsened with each of her eighteen pregnancies, including seven miscarriages.

Like Sanger's mother, the women with whom she worked had no access to contraception. Pharmacists and midwives refused to give women information about birth control for fear of arrest. Whispered advice about what to do when a woman or girl found herself facing an unwanted pregnancy included drinking turpentine, rolling down the stairs, or inserting knitting needles into the uterus to bring on sponta- neous abortion. "On Saturday nights," Sanger later wrote in her autobiography, "I have seen groups of from fifty to one hundred [women] with their shawls over their heads waiting outside the office of a five-dollar abortionist." She added, "Pregnancy was a chronic condition among the women of this [working] class."

In July 1912, a doctor telephoned Sanger to ask for her help with the case of Sadie Sachs, a married woman in her late twenties. Sachs lay on the floor, unconscious from a self-induced abortion. Her three crying children and her husband, Jake, stood helpless around her. For three weeks, Sanger nursed Sachs back to health. When the doctor paid one last visit, he warned Sachs, "Any more such capers [self-induced abortions], young woman, and there'll be no need to send for me."

"I know, doctor," Sachs said, "but what can I do to prevent it?"

"Tell Jake to sleep on the roof," he said, as he departed.

Three months later, Jake Sachs telephoned Sanger. He begged her to come

Margaret Sanger (*above*) was a revolutionary in the struggle for women's reproductive rights. She and her sister, Ethel Byrne, opened the nation's first birth control clinic, in New York City, in 1916. This photo at a train station in Chicago was taken the next year.

quickly. His wife had induced another abortion. When Sanger arrived, Sadie Sachs slipped into a coma and died.

Many historians think that Sanger exaggerated the story of Sadie Sachs. If so, her tale about the doctor's unwillingness to provide meaningful contraceptive advice was meant to emphasize an important point. Poor women in the United States had limited or no access to reproductive control. If they found themselves with an unwanted pregnancy, they could not afford safe abortions.

THE *NEW YORK CALL* AND THE *WOMAN REBEL*

Sanger and her husband were Socialists and belonged to the Socialist Party of America. (Socialism is a political philosophy that promotes government ownership or oversight of a community's main industries.) The Sangers helped laborers organize strikes for higher wages and better working conditions. However, the Socialist Party's lack of interest in women's issues frustrated Sanger, who wanted to better women's lives. She looked to the political ideas of Emma Goldman, an American feminist, anarchist, and radical thinker. Goldman advocated absolute personal freedom of speech, workers' and women's rights, and sexual and reproductive freedom. Sanger began to adopt many of Goldman's positions on the need for women to take charge of their own identities and of their bodies.

One night in 1912, an editor from the *New York Call*, a Socialist daily newspaper, asked Sanger to speak to a group of women about workers' rights because the scheduled lecturer had canceled. Sanger, "shaking and quaking," spoke to the small group of women in the first public speech she had ever made in her life. She did not feel qualified to speak about workers' rights, so she picked a topic that was dear to her: female health. The women in Sanger's audience asked questions about sexual intimacy and reproductive control that inspired the *New York Call* to publish a weekly column by Sanger. The column, "What Every Girl Should Know," discussed issues including sex, pregnancy, and abortion.

Anthony Comstock struck out against Sanger's columns. As an agent of the NYSSV and of the US Postal Service, he ordered the *New York Call* not to publish a column that discussed STDs. To protest the censorship, the newspaper printed a defiant headline in place of Sanger's column:

"What Every Girl Should Know—Nothing; By Order of the Post-Office Department." According to Sanger biographer Ellen Chesler, the *New York Call* successfully fought the Postal Service's order and Sanger's banned article was published in the paper several weeks later.

Sanger was furious about the suppression of her column. She decided to challenge the Comstock Act by continuing to publish articles about birth control. In 1914 she began publishing the *Woman Rebel*, a monthly journal advocating equality between spouses and birth control, a term she coined. The Postal Service banned three issues of the journal, and the US government then prosecuted Sanger under the Comstock Act.

"But I myself had no intention of going to jail; it was not in *my* program," Sanger later wrote. "Parting from all that I held dear in life, I left New York at midnight, without a passport, not knowing whether I could ever return."

Sanger fled to England, where she met many radical thinkers who influenced her thoughts about sexual freedom and birth control. In Holland she visited Dr. Johannes Rutgers, who helped run a nationwide system of birth control clinics. Rutgers convinced Sanger of the superiority of diaphragms over cervical caps and other pessaries. Because proper use of the diaphragm required a physician to measure and fit each individual woman, the device was safer and more reliable. Sanger's new preference for the diaphragm would forever influence the direction she would take on birth control. For the diaphragm to be widely distributed in the United States, however, Sanger would have to gain the medical community's approval of the new technique. She would also have to increase women's access to physician-assisted reproductive health care. US obscenity laws and Americans' uneasiness with female contraception would make both difficult to achieve.

When Sanger's husband, Bill, was sentenced to thirty days in jail for distributing *Family Limitation*, a pamphlet Sanger had written about birth control, she decided it was time to sail home and face trial. However, Sanger never had her day in court. In November 1915, Sanger's daughter Peggy died suddenly, and the judge, in sympathy, dropped the charges.

MARY WARE DENNETT

While Sanger was abroad, Mary Ware Dennett became a strong presence in the American birth control movement. In 1915 she and a group of women in New York City formed the National Birth Control League (NBCL), the first US birth control organization to fight for changes to state and federal obscenity laws. The NBCL's motto was "The first right a child should have is that of being wanted."

Dennett and Sanger did not get along personally, and they disagreed on strategy. For example, Dennett disapproved of Sanger's radical tactic of fighting for rights by flaunting the law and risking imprisonment. At the time, even liberal freethinkers such as Emma Goldman feared that Sanger's combative style was alienating many Americans who might otherwise support birth control. Dennett thought conciliation and lobbying would accomplish more than Sanger's direct confrontation with the law. Sanger viewed birth control as a woman's sole responsibility. But Dennett thought good parenting required that both men and women take responsibility for bringing a child into the world. In addition, Sanger's public airing of her mother's birthing difficulties and impoverished background irritated Dennett, who came from an upper-middle-class family. Dennett, who was reluctant to reveal private matters, had her own personal reasons for supporting contraception. She had survived three difficult births and had had a child who died as an infant. Even with these hardships, Dennett could not get information about contraception from her doctors. For Sanger's part, she considered herself the pioneer of the birth control movement. She did not want to share the limelight with Dennett or the NBCL.

Dennett was a force for Sanger to deal with. When the NBCL disbanded in 1919 because of a lack of funding,

Mary Ware Dennett *(center)* was a leader in the fight for women's right to vote in the early part of the twentieth century. She is, however, better known for establishing the National Birth Control League in 1915, an organization dedicated to overturning obscenity laws and to providing information about birth control. This photo was taken in 1913.

Dennett immediately established the Voluntary Parenthood League (VPL). From 1919 to 1926, the VPL vigorously lobbied Congress to remove the words "prevention of conception" from the Comstock Act. Without those words in the law, contraceptive information and products could be legally shared with and available to everyone, and even a physician's prescription would be unnecessary. Mothers could mail contraceptive material to their daughters, and high school teachers could talk about reproduction with their students. Teens, Dennett thought, should understand the science of reproduction and the sex act in the context of a loving relationship. As biographer Constance M. Chen noted, "Ultimately, Dennett's goal was to eliminate fear and shame about sex."

Sanger argued instead for the right of doctors to legally discuss and dispense contraception, mostly diaphragms, to women for health purposes. Without a doctor's involvement, Sanger feared, the public would be misled about safe and reliable contraceptive methods. By siding with medical doctors, Sanger hoped to increase awareness of the importance of birth control and to help legalize it. For her part, Dennett viewed Sanger's "doctors-only bill" as legislation for the upper classes, since many poor women could not afford to visit a doctor. She also thought it would suppress free speech by legalizing only birth control conversations between a woman and her doctor.

A BIRTH CONTROL CLINIC AND A HUNGER STRIKE

Impatient with the slow pace of reform, Sanger decided to directly challenge Sections 1142 and 1145 of the New York Penal Code. Section 1142 made it unlawful for a person to spread information or medicine "for the prevention of conception." Section 1145, though, carved out an exception. It allowed physicians to prescribe birth control "for the cure or prevention of disease."

To Sanger's chagrin, doctors had been applying the exception only to men who wanted protection from STDs. She wanted to make sure doctors would also apply the exception to women whose health was at risk from too many pregnancies. She felt that women, like men, should "have the right to control their own destinies."

Sanger searched for a doctor to help her open a birth control clinic. Opening such a clinic would have been illegal at the time, and she could find no one willing to risk arrest. So Sanger worked with her sister, Ethel Byrne, also a nurse, to open the first birth control clinic in the United States.

On October 16, 1916, Sanger and Byrne defied the law

by opening a birth control clinic in the Brownsville section of Brooklyn, New York. That morning about 150 women stood in line, many with their children. The clinic remained open for nine days until a policewoman, posing as a patient, arrested Sanger; Byrne; and an assistant, Fania Mindell, and carted them off to the police station.

Byrne was brought to trial on January 8, 1917. The judge sentenced her to thirty days in jail. In protest, Byrne began a hunger strike. Each day she grew steadily weaker. Finally, after Byrne had refused food and drink for four days, Commissioner of Correction Burdette Lewis ordered her to be force-fed through a rubber tube inserted into her mouth.

Sanger wrote daily press releases about Byrne's declining health. Newspapers featured front-page headlines such as

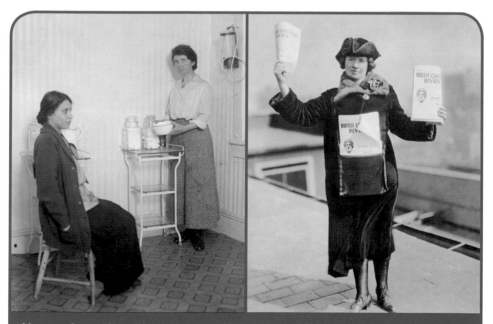

Margaret Sanger *(standing, in photo at left)* attends to a patient at her birth control clinic in New York City around the year 1920. Besides running the clinic, Sanger also published and edited the *Birth Control Review* as a forum for discussing reproductive issues in print. Political activist Kitty Marion *(photo at right)* sold the magazine for twenty cents a copy on street corners in New York. She faced death threats, physical abuse, and police harassment.

"Mrs. Byrne Sinking Fast Sister Warns" and "Mrs. Byrne Now Fed By Force." In interviews, Lewis shot back, declaring, "If Mrs. Sanger is as careful of the facts when she is [spreading] knowledge of birth control as she appears to be when she says her sister is in a state of coma, I should say that her advice was not worth much." After Byrne had served twenty days in jail, New York governor Charles Whitman pardoned her on the condition that she would not engage in unlawful activity again. An ambulance transported the ailing Byrne to Sanger's house.

The night before Sanger's own trial began, three thousand women rallied in Manhattan's Carnegie Hall to show their support and to protest the New York law. At the gathering, Mary Ware Dennett joined a group of women called the Committee of 100, who had formed to protest the clinic arrests. Sanger also sold the first copies of her newest monthly journal, the *Birth Control Review*, at the meeting. For decades the journal served to educate readers about the birth control movement in the United States.

Sanger was sentenced to one month in jail, but she appealed her case. Appeals court judge Frederick Crane upheld Sanger's conviction in 1918. Sanger was triumphant, however. Judge Crane's ruling expanded the meaning of the term *disease* in the physicians' exception in Section 1145 to include dangerous pregnancies. Then, with a physician's prescription in hand, women could lawfully obtain contraceptives from pharmacists to prevent dangerous pregnancies.

Ironically, Crane's ruling increased sales of male contraceptives. Manufacturers of condoms would market the products "for the prevention of disease only," even though they were used for birth control. And although Crane's ruling legalized condom sales only with a doctor's prescription, this requirement was routinely overlooked. As a result, barber-shops, newsstands, and gas stations began openly selling condoms in large numbers. Sanger recognized that male contraceptives were better than no protection at all. But she was disappointed that women had to rely on men to avoid pregnancy. "No woman could call herself free who does not own and control her own body," she wrote.

For Sanger, Crane's ruling gave her the green light to open the Birth Control Clinical Research Bureau (BCCRB) in New York City in January 1923. With the backing of the American Birth Control League (ABCL), an advocacy group she had established in 1921, Sanger staffed the clinic with doctors and social workers. Women in New York then had a place to go to get a doctor's prescription for contraception, usually diaphragms. They could also receive a wide range of reproductive health services, from annual checkups to renewals of prescriptions. Within a few years, clinics opened in Baltimore, Chicago, Cleveland, Detroit, Los Angeles, Newark, and San Francisco. Through the ABCL, Sanger also hired Dr. James Cooper to educate other physicians about contraceptive techniques. In 1927 Cooper visited almost every state in the country and lined up volunteers, nurses, social workers, and businessmen to support and help fund ABCL-affiliated clinics. American women then had a greater measure of control over their reproduction.

EUGENICS FEVER

As immigration to the United States rose in the 1920s and white birthrates began to drop, the eugenics movement gained strength. Eugenicists feared that nonwhite peoples, whom they viewed as inferior, would overtake the white, native-born American population.

By the early twentieth century, the US military was looking for ways to deal with the large numbers of soldiers who were contracting STDs through encounters with prostitutes while on duty at home and overseas. One approach was to distribute pro-kits (prophylactic, or contraception, kits) to the soldiers. Moral reformers, though, believed this encouraged men to have sex outside of marriage. "It's wicked," US secretary of the navy Josephus Daniels wrote in 1915, referring to the distribution of pro-kits with ointments for men to use after having sex with someone they suspected of having a venereal disease. The kits, he warned "will lead them [sailors] to think they may indulge in practices which are not sanctioned [approved] by moral, military or civil law." In 1915 he banned the pro-kits and, instead, urged men in the navy to practice abstinence.

US secretary of war Newton Baker, who also advocated abstinence, stressed "education prophylaxis," or teaching solders about sexual hygiene. On April 17, 1917, eleven days after the United States entered World War I (1914–1918), Baker established the Commission on Training Camp Activities (CTCA) to educate soldiers about good hygiene and STDs. The CTCA's most popular pamphlet, "Keeping Fit to Fight," stressed a soldier's patriotic duty to stay healthy and free of STDs.

During World War I, General John J. Pershing issued General Order No. 6, which required soldiers to report for treatment within three hours of having sexual intercourse. For the first time ever, a soldier with an STD could face a court-martial. Even so, approximately 380,000 US troops were infected with STDs from April 1917 to December 1919.

In the 1930s, the military changed its views on abstinence, approving condoms for disease prevention. Recognizing that servicemen were sexually active, and looking to prevent widespread transmission of STDs, the military branches distributed about fifty million condoms a month to servicemen during World War II (1939–1945).

During the war, the US Congress passed legislation to establish a women's corps in each branch of the armed forces. Women's Army

During World War II, the US military, the US Surgeon General's office, and the War Advertising Council collaborated to produce a series of propaganda posters to inform the public and US soldiers about the risks of venereal, or sexually transmitted, diseases. This poster from World War II notes the dangers and promotes the use of prophylaxis for safe sex.

Corps (WAC) colonel Oveta Culp Hobby sought to portray the WAC as "chaste and asexual." Her view conflicted with the goals of US surgeon general Thomas Parran Jr., who was committed to wiping out STDs in the military. When Parran tried to launch sex education and promote birth control for the WAC and to place condom vending machines in female bathrooms, Hobby balked. Secretary of War Henry Stimson, bowing to Hobby's pressure, ordered that women be denied contraception. In the end, military rules for men and women were contradictory. For example, WAC members and servicemen frequently dated, even when regulations prohibited socialization. When men and women were caught breaking the rules, men were rarely punished while women could be discharged from the WAC.

Sterilization Laws

In 1923 seventeen-year-old Virginian Carrie Buck was raped and became pregnant. After she gave birth, authorities claimed that Carrie's baby was "an illegitimate feeble-minded child" and that Buck should be sterilized. She challenged Virginia's law authorizing forced sterilization for "socially inadequate person[s]." In 1927 the US Supreme Court case *Buck v. Bell* upheld Virginia's sterilization law. Justice Oliver Wendell Holmes wrote that states had a right to enact laws that protected the public health, including protecting against the spread of inherited mental deficiency. He declared, "Three generations of imbeciles [in the Buck family] are enough." Buck was therefore involuntarily sterilized.

Holmes's ruling sparked other states to enact forced sterilization laws for people with conditions such as mental retardation and insanity, which were then believed to be inherited. By mid-century, thirty-two states had sterilization laws. The seventy thousand people sterilized until the 1970s included many more women than men. Most of the people sterilized were poor black women, many of whom had borne children outside of marriage.

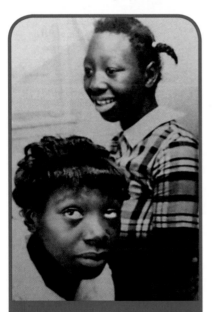

Involuntary sterilization continued well into the late 1900s. In 1973 the Southern Poverty Law Center sued the US Department of Health, Education, and Welfare for the involuntary sterilization of Minnie and Mary Alice Relf *(above)*. The lawsuit led to the requirement that doctors obtain informed consent for all sterilization procedures.

In *Skinner v. State of Oklahoma* (1942), the US Supreme Court modified its earlier position on sterilization in *Buck v. Bell*. The court ruled that an Oklahoma statute (law) authorizing sterilization for criminals convicted of three felonies was unconstitutional. In the decision, Justice William O. Douglas stated, "We are dealing here with legislation which involves one of the basic civil rights of man. Marriage and procreation are fundamental to the very existence and survival of the race."

Americans who supported eugenics were in favor of breeding what they thought of as healthy, fit children with good genes that would be passed down through generations. They supported sterilization to limit and control the reproduction of the people they viewed as unfit. Unfit Americans, in the minds of eugenicists, included the poor, the mentally retarded, those with low intelligence, the insane, criminals, and alcoholics. Eugenicists targeted African Americans, whom they viewed as lacking in intelligence. They also targeted immigrants from eastern and southern Europe, whom they blamed for an increase in crime.

Margaret Sanger liked the idea of eugenics as a scientific theory. She was not alone in thinking this way. Many prominent Americans, including former US president Theodore Roosevelt and Harvard University president Charles Eliot, spoke out in favor of eugenics. Sanger decided to link her cause with eugenics as a way to promote birth control. Sanger did not promote positive eugenics, or the encouragement of breeding between people viewed as the fittest. She did, however, champion a form of negative eugenics, which involved limiting the reproduction of mentally deficient people. For these people and for those "afflicted with inherited or transmissible diseases," Sanger urged "encouragement" of sterilization.

Sanger never directly advocated racism or the idea that lower-class people carried inferior genes, as did many supporters of eugenics. Instead, she blamed poverty, not genes or race, for criminality and for poor intellectual development among children. She urged contraception as a way to lower birthrates among poor families. But when she spoke publicly of the use of contraception to create a "race of thoroughbreds," her words gave the impression of promoting

BETTER HEALTH for 13,000,000

THE RESULTS OF A TWO-YEAR EXPERIMENT TO DEMONSTRATE THAT AN OFTEN NEGLECTED BUT FUNDAMENTAL PHASE OF PREVENTIVE MEDICINE CAN BE MADE A PROFITABLE PART OF EVERY PUBLIC HEALTH PROGRAM

The cover of a 1943 Planned Parenthood pamphlet highlights four black teens. Black Americans have historically been divided about Planned Parenthood and birth control efforts in general. In the early decades of the twentieth century, many suspected racism and were suspicious of the support of eugenics among birth control leaders. Many blacks feared that birth control was deliberately aimed at limiting birthrates among black Americans. Other African Americans supported the effort to educate all Americans about reproductive health.

racial superiority and of prejudice against lower classes. In segregated American society, where black people were seen as inferior, Sanger's words enforced the idea that reproduction among black people should be controlled and limited.

RELIGIOUS INFLUENCES

By the 1930s, many religious groups, including the Anglican Church, Universalists, Unitarians, liberal Protestant sects, and Reform Jews, had endorsed birth control devices and methods to varying degrees. But the Catholic Church vehemently opposed artificial birth control. In 1930 Pope Pius XI—the head of the Roman Catholic Church—sent a letter, known as an encyclical, to all Catholic bishops. The encyclical, called the *Casti Connubii* (Latin for "of chaste marriage"), declared that all forms of artificial birth control were against Catholic teachings. The pope also condemned women's increasing freedom and proclaimed that wives were subjected to the rule of their husbands.

Catholic Church officials promoted the use of the rhythm method for those Catholics who wanted to limit the size of their families. Thousands of Catholic couples began using the rythm method, which in just a few years physicians would deem unreliable.

Christian Marriage

By His Holiness Pope Pius XI

POPE PIUS XI

LONDON
CATHOLIC TRUTH SOCIETY
3b/40. Eccleston Square, S.W.1, and 28a Ashley Place, S.W.1
Branches at Liverpool, Manchester, Birmingham, Brighton, Cardiff, Newcastle, and Derby
Price Twopence

The encyclical letter *Casti Connubii,* or "of chaste marriage," from Pope Pius XI—the head of the Roman Catholic Church at the time—forbade abortion and all forms of artificial birth control. While holding firm to traditional, conservative Catholic values, the encyclical did also speak out against eugenics.

GUTTING THE COMSTOCK ACT

During the economic downturn of the Great Depression (1929–1942), many Americans longed for reliable contraception to keep their families small. Millions of workers had lost their jobs and could not afford to support even a small family. As one married woman from Saint Louis, Missouri, wrote in a 1936 letter to Sanger: "We have a darling baby girl that we love dearly. . . . He [her husband] makes $18.00 a week, that isn't much but we are happy that it is that much. . . . I am so sick & nervous & always worried about getting pregnant." For many women, anxiety led to desperation. About one million abortions were performed yearly during the early 1930s.

Three federal decisions paved the way for legalization of birth control. Mary Ware Dennett set the stage by challenging the federal obscenity laws with a sex education pamphlet called *The Sex Side of Life: An Explanation for Young People.* Dennett had written the pamphlet in 1915, when her son started asking questions about sex. After combing the library and bookstores for appropriate sex education information for teens, she noted that the available material spoke "as if the sex relation was *in itself* a *wrong* thing—to be suppressed or ashamed of." Nothing she read "explain[ed] carefully enough *just what* the sex act is." Authors, Dennett wrote, assume "that people know what it is and how it should be done and when etc. but they don't." By using straightforward language and illustrations of the male and female sex organs in her pamphlet, Dennett explained sexual intercourse as an expression of love during marriage.

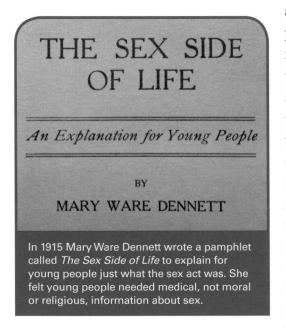

THE SEX SIDE
OF LIFE

An Explanation for Young People

BY

MARY WARE DENNETT

In 1915 Mary Ware Dennett wrote a pamphlet called *The Sex Side of Life* to explain for young people just what the sex act was. She felt young people needed medical, not moral or religious, information about sex.

Years later, in 1929, Dennett went to trial for mailing her pamphlet to a woman who requested a copy. By that time, she had already sold twenty-five thousand copies to a wide range of buyers, including the YMCA; public health departments; hundreds of welfare and religious groups; professors; doctors; and the public schools of Bronxville, New York. "If I have corrupted the youth of America," Dennett declared when she was sentenced in court to a fine of $300, "a year in jail is not enough for me. And I will not pay the fine!" Her stance brought her instant fame. In an interview with the *New York Times*, she pronounced, "I shall carry this to the Supreme Court, if necessary. I have no intention of abandoning my principles."

When the case reached his court on appeal, Judge Augustus Hand found that "an accurate [explanation] of the relevant facts of the sex side of life in decent language . . . cannot . . . be regarded as obscene." The ruling was important. After the Dennett case, information about sex was no longer considered obscene in the United States.

In a second case, *Youngs Rubber Corporation v. C. I. Lee & Co.* (1930), New York federal appeals court judge Thomas Swan decided in favor of the right of manufacturers to transport and sell condoms directly to drugstores without the need for prescriptions from doctors. Otherwise, the judge reasoned, druggists would have no way to obtain condoms to fill patient prescriptions in the first place. Swan ruled that selling condoms to drugstores was legal if "they are prescribed [to a patient] by a physician for the prevention of disease, or for the prevention of conception, where that is not forbidden by local law."

Even with these legal victories, Sanger still longed for a legal ruling to support the medical exemption in the Comstock Act. In 1936 she decided to force the issue. She arranged for the shipment of 120 pessaries from Japan to a physician, Dr. Hannah Stone, the director of the Birth Control Clinical Research Bureau, so Stone could prescribe diaphragms for medical purposes in the clinic. US Customs officials seized the shipment. Stone was charged with violating the Tariff Act by importing articles from Japan "for the prevention of conception." In the 1936 case *United States v. One Package,* a New York federal appeals court ordered US Customs to release the pessaries. Sanger and birth control advocates had won a momentous victory.

The *One Package* ruling, also made by Judge Augustus Hand, held that outlawing items viewed as immoral in 1873 no longer applied in modern-day 1936. Hand reasoned that Congress would not have "denounced [contraceptive articles] as immoral if it had understood all the conditions under which they were to be used." The court stated that those conditions included instances when contraceptive items "might intelligently be [used] by . . . competent physicians for the purpose of saving life or promoting the well being of their patients."

After more than sixty years, the Comstock Act's provision that contraceptive articles were obscene had been gutted. Once again, Sanger made headline news in major newspapers and magazines. In accepting a medal "for her pioneer work in behalf of birth control" from the Town Hall Club of New York, Sanger said, "The greatest obstacle to prevent needless sacrifice of women's lives, the suffering, the mental agony, the damaged bodies were the Federal laws which had been placed on the statute books and tied up the whole subject of birth control with that of obscenity."

WARTIME AND REPRODUCTIVE RIGHTS

Three years later, in 1939, the ABCL and the BCCRB joined forces and became the Birth Control Federation of America, later named the Planned Parenthood Federation of America (PPFA). As more women took leadership positions in the movement, Sanger retired to Tucson, Arizona. After World War II, population control issues spurred Sanger to rejoin the fight for birth control, this time in underdeveloped countries.

But Sanger's contraceptive method of choice—the diaphragm—never really caught on. Because the device was expensive, only a small minority of well-to-do women purchased it. Women complained that insertion of the diaphragm with the required spermicidal jelly was difficult and messy. In addition, when women consulted their doctors for contraceptive advice, the diaphragm was not widely recommended. Many doctors remained untrained in how to properly fit it. Instead, couples frequently used condoms, and women bought over-the-counter feminine hygiene products. In the 1930s and 1940s, manufacturers aggressively advertised chemical douches, such as Lysol disinfectant, in women's magazines under titles such as "Can a Married Woman Ever Feel Safe?" and "The Fear That 'Blights' Romance and Ages Women Prematurely." Women exposed themselves to serious infection and even death from products that turned out to be unreliable as contraceptives.

In an important ruling during the war, the US Supreme Court declared in 1942 that conceiving and giving birth to children were fundamental human rights. And most Americans still viewed reproduction as their natural duty. Many women worked, especially during the war years. Yet those who stayed home, had babies, and took care of their families were viewed with more respect. For married men, stay-at-home wives were status symbols that showed men had enough money to support stay-at-home families. Even with the court's ruling, however, reproductive rights were handled unequally and hinged on whether a woman was married or not. For example, 40 percent of states had laws

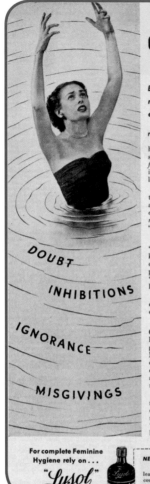

TOO LATE TO CRY OUT IN ANGUISH!

Beware of the one intimate neglect that can engulf you in marital grief

TOO LATE, when love has gone, for a wife to plead that no one warned her of danger. Because a wise, considerate wife makes it her business to *find out* how to safeguard her daintiness in order to protect precious married love and happiness.

One of the soundest ways for a wife to keep married love in bloom is to achieve dainty allure by practicing *effective* feminine hygiene such as *regular* vaginal douches with reliable "Lysol."

Germs destroyed swiftly

"Lysol" has amazing, *proved* power to kill germ-life on contact . . . truly cleanses the vaginal canal even in the presence of mucous matter. Thus "Lysol" *acts* in a way that makeshifts like soap, salt or soda *never can*.

Appealing daintiness is assured, because the very source of objectionable odors is eliminated.

Use whenever needed!

Gentle, non-caustic "Lysol" will not harm delicate tissue. Easy directions give correct douching solution. Many doctors advise their patients to douche regularly with "Lysol" brand disinfectant, just to insure daintiness alone, and to use it as often as they need it. No greasy aftereffect.

For feminine hygiene, three times more women use "Lysol" than any other liquid preparation. No other is more reliable. You, too, can rely on "Lysol" to help protect your married happiness . . . keep you desirable!

DOUBT

INHIBITIONS

IGNORANCE

MISGIVINGS

For complete Feminine Hygiene rely on . . . "*Lysol*" Brand Disinfectant

NEW! . . . FEMININE HYGIENE FACTS!
FREE! New booklet of information by leading gynecological authority. Mail coupon to Lehn & Fink, 192 Bloomfield Avenue, Bloomfield, N. J.

This 1950s ad for Lysol disinfectant pushes women to use the product as part of a regular douching routine. Like other Lysol ads from the 1940s to the 1960s, this one suggests that Lysol douching is a key part of any stable marriage. Lysol was the most common form of birth control during this period, even though it was largely ineffective and was known to cause burning, inflammation, and even death.

that prohibited welfare payments to families in which children were born outside of marriage. Payments were also denied when social workers found evidence of a mother living with or having sexual relations with a man outside of marriage. These laws were directed at both poor white women and poor black women. However, states typically enforced them only against black mothers. As historian Rickie Solinger notes, in practical terms, privacy in sexual and family relationships was reserved for married white women with money.

Women who faced an unwanted pregnancy during the war years continued to seek abortions. When a pregnancy threatened a woman's emotional or physical health, showed evidence of fetal abnormalities, or was the result of rape or incest, so-called therapeutic abortions were legal.

During the late 1940s and the 1950s, doctors formed hospital committees to determine which women were eligible for such abortions. (The committees operated through the 1960s.) Women seeking the abortions were required to appear before an all-male group to plead their cases. Many women who were granted abortions were also forced to agree to sterilization at the same time. This practice punished women for what the medical community viewed as irresponsible sexual behavior. It also ensured that the women would not be back for repeat abortions. As one doctor noted, "[It's] as if the physician is saying, 'All right, if you do not want this baby, you are not capable of having any.'"

According to studies in the early 1950s, "More than 53 percent of teaching hospitals made simultaneous sterilization a condition of approval for abortion, and in all U.S. hospitals, the rate [of sterilization] was 40 percent." Fearful of losing control over their ability to bear children in the future, many women therefore sought illegal and unsafe abortions.

All the same, World War II brought big changes to American society. Women had joined the workforce in larger numbers than ever before. With wartime jobs, women got a taste of financial power and independence. Soldiers came home with a broader sense of the world and its many freedoms. As a result, sexual attitudes began to loosen, and women and men were more willing to have sex for pleasure and outside of marriage. Yet without the safety net of legal

The Racial Politics of Out-of-Wedlock Pregnancy

Young women of all races have become pregnant outside of marriage. In the first several decades of the twentieth century, mainstream society considered them all to be "deviants."

Families dealt very differently with these pregnancies. Black mothers, for example, rarely gave up their babies. They raised their children, usually with the support and guidance of their families and community. When public assistance became available in the 1940s and 1950s, large numbers of poor unmarried black women sought the help for themselves and their children. Meanwhile, politicians began to portray these women as sexually promiscuous, irresponsible mothers, who bore children only to receive welfare payments. Segregationists built on this attitude to fuel their belief that separate schools for black students and white students were necessary. They claimed that the children of unwed black mothers would spread bad values to white students if schools were racially mixed.

In white families, unmarried pregnant girls and women were considered "unfit to be mothers." Families were ashamed of their pregnant daughters and sent them away to temporary homes, far from their neighborhoods, to keep the pregnancies secret. After the girls and women gave birth, white couples adopted the babies, often without the mothers' consent. Historian Rickie Solinger has noted that a young unmarried pregnant woman "redeemed herself" by adopting out her baby. She could then return home without the stigma of single motherhood.

and reliable birth control and abortion, women were still walking a dangerous tightrope.

Sanger, Dennett, and birth control advocates had fought hard for contraception in the years leading up to the war, and US courts were slowly acknowledging the contraceptive needs of women. Yet American government and society remained far from accepting reproductive freedom as a fundamental human right. Conditions were ripe for something big to happen.

CHAPTER 5
BREAKTHROUGH: THE PILL

Multimillionaire Stanley McCormick, heir to a family fortune built on agricultural machinery, died in 1947. He left his immense wealth to his wife, Katharine. A biologist and suffragist, she decided to pour the money into finding a new contraceptive method for women that was quick and easy to use. At the time, scientists were discovering many wonder drugs, vaccines, and treatments for life-threatening diseases. Why, McCormick wondered, couldn't someone develop a birth control pill?

Katharine McCormick and Margaret Sanger had been corresponding for several years about birth control issues. In 1950, with her late husband's fortune in hand, McCormick wrote to Sanger to say she would help fund birth control research. With this financial support, Sanger's dream of a "magic pill" for birth control might actually come true.

Sanger had someone in mind to spearhead the research: Dr. Gregory Pincus, a biologist with expertise in reproduction whom she met at a dinner party in 1951. In 1952 Pincus teamed with physician and fertility expert Dr. John Rock, from Shrewsbury, Massachusetts, who was conducting research on sterility. Although he was Catholic, Rock believed in birth control for women, particularly when their health was in danger. Rock agreed to run the clinical trials required by the US Food and Drug Administration before any pill could be approved for sale.

Katharine McCormick *(left)* was a suffragist and a leader in the reproductive health movement in the United States. In this photo dating to July 1914, she sails to a suffrage convention in Europe. Years later, she worked with Dr. Gregory Pincus *(right)* to develop the birth control pill, which reached the market in 1960. In this 1962 photo, Pincus dips a container of eggs into a hormone solution as part of an experiment to change the sex of the unhatched chicks. By this time, Pincus was heading the birth defects research program at the Worcester Foundation for Experimental Biology in Massachusetts.

In June 1953, Sanger and McCormick met Pincus at the Worcester Foundation for Experimental Biology, his lab in Worcester, Massachusetts. McCormick was so impressed with Pincus and so convinced that he would succeed in the quest to develop a pill that she wrote him a generous check for $40,000 on the spot.

From the day she met Pincus, McCormick actively followed the lab's work. She played a key role in encouraging the research, pushing Pincus and his team to begin clinical trials, and keeping Sanger informed of progress. McCormick even moved from Santa Barbara, California, to Boston to keep close contact with the Massachusetts scientists. And when Rock began clinical trials, McCormick followed his work every step of the way.

Katharine McCormick

Katharine McCormick was a very unusual woman for her time. In 1904, when most women did not attend college, she graduated from the Massachusetts Institute of Technology with a degree in biology. When she met Margaret Sanger at a talk in Boston in 1917, McCormick was already an avid supporter of women's suffrage. She financed the *Woman's Journal*, a publication advocating women's voting rights, and was vice president of the National American Woman Suffrage Association (NAWSA). After women were granted the right to vote in 1920, she helped establish and was vice president of the League of Women Voters, a group seeking to educate women about the importance of voting.

Katharine McCormick *(left)* and Mrs. Charles Parker hold a NAWSA banner at the 1913 National American Woman Suffrage Association convention in Washington, DC.

McCormick strongly believed in Sanger's cause because of a tragedy in her own life. Her husband had been diagnosed with schizophrenia shortly after they were married. Fearing that the disease was hereditary, she decided not to have children. She eventually donated a total of $2 million toward developing a birth control pill. In fact, aside from initial grants of money from the PPFA, the research and development work that led to the Pill was entirely funded by private donations from McCormick.

Pincus and his collaborator Min-Chueh Chang, who studied sperm and the reproduction of mammals, thought that the clue to developing a pill lay in figuring out how to stop ovulation. When a woman does not ovulate, sperm released by her partner during sex have nothing to fertilize and the woman cannot become pregnant. Pincus and Chang thought that the hormone progesterone alone would prevent pregnancy by stopping ovulation. Progesterone also prevents egg fertilization. It thickens the mucus in the cervix so that sperm cannot travel into the uterus. It also creates an unfriendly environment for the egg by preventing the growth of the uterine lining, to which a fertilized egg must attach to create a pregnancy.

The answer to avoiding pregnancy, though, turned out to be a combination of two hormones that are released naturally during a woman's reproductive cycle—estrogen and progesterone. Rock and Pincus developed a pill that released these hormones to stop a woman's natural ovulation cycle. The pill had to be taken every day to be effective.

Rock first tested the pill on women in his own medical practice and on volunteer nurses. In later trials, though, he chose women who were not required by law to give legal consent. They included psychiatric patients at Worcester State Hospital outside of Boston and minority women in Puerto Rico and Haiti. Rock was later criticized for the unethical aspects of choosing vulnerable and poor women for these trials, although his work was in keeping with the practice of medical experimentation at the time.

ENOVID

Pincus initially approached G. D. Searle, a pharmaceutical company in Skokie, Illinois, to develop and market the

Developing a "Magic Pill"

Pincus and Rock are often referred to as the inventors of the Pill. Yet other chemists pioneered key components that jump-started the Pill's development. In the first half of the twentieth century, scientists experimented with the hormones estrogen and progesterone to help women who wanted to get pregnant but couldn't and to help women with painful or extra-long periods of menstruation. At the time, these hormones could only be extracted from dead animals, a very expensive process.

The first big breakthrough came when chemist Russell Marker made progesterone from a chemical found in yams in the 1930s. Marker's formulation was less costly, but it could only be given in painful injections. Then, in the early 1950s, chemists Carl Djerassi and Frank Colton each separately invented an oral version of synthetic (artificial) progesterone. Pincus was elated. He needed synthetic progesterone that could be used in pill form, and then it became available. Searle won the race for bringing the Pill to the market in 1960. Djerassi's synthetic progesterone was eventually used in a birth control pill manufactured by a Mexican pharmaceutical company, Syntex, which began to market its pill in the United States in 1962.

contraceptive pill in the United States. However, Searle was unwilling to provide complete financial support for Pincus because he had failed to perfect a medication the company had funded several years earlier. As a result, Searle agreed to provide Pincus with only the necessary chemical compounds to test the pill in clinical trials. Even when the scientists began to report encouraging results from the experiments in the mid-1950s, the company still refused to back the project. At the time, thirty states still outlawed the advertising and sale of birth control. In this climate, Searle was reluctant to get too involved. The company feared backlash from the Catholic Church and assumed that women would not want to buy a pill they would have to take every day. Searle permitted Pincus to publish favorable results from the Puerto Rico trials in 1957. But the company stressed that it wanted "to avoid our being associated, even by implication," with a contraceptive pill. So news of the pill's breakthrough appeared in magazines such as *Reader's Digest* and *Ladies' Home Journal* without reference to Searle. The news created a wave of excitement in the public. By the late 1950s, Searle was ready to take a risk and began manufacturing a birth control pill called Enovid.

In 1957 the FDA approved Enovid, but only for gynecological problems such as excessive menstruation. (Menstruation is the body's method of shedding unfertilized eggs. By limiting ovulation, the pill would limit menstruation as well.) McCormick and Sanger were ecstatic. They knew that once the FDA approved a drug, doctors could lawfully prescribe it for other off-label conditions—that is, conditions the drug was not intended for but that it could successfully treat. And that's exactly what occurred. Across the country, thousands of women got wind of the new pill that could prevent pregnancy. Patients flooded their doctors' offices for prescriptions for the birth control pill, and by the end of 1959, doctors had prescribed Enovid to half a million women.

Pincus received volumes of fan mail from women who shared their gratitude. An executive secretary of a Planned Parenthood clinic in Saint Paul, Minnesota, wrote to tell him about a woman who "has 'kissed' your picture (in our local newspaper)—she is so grateful to you, for this is the first year in her eight years of marriage that she has not been pregnant."

In May 1960, the FDA officially approved Enovid for birth control purposes. Within five years, more than six million women in the United States were taking Enovid and other oral birth control pills. By 1967 the number of women on oral birth control pills had jumped to approximately 12.8 million worldwide. With one tiny pill, women and their male partners could avoid the mess of spermicides, the awkwardness of diaphragms, and the unreliability of condoms and the rhythm method. The monumental effect of the drug was reflected in its simple nickname: the Pill.

"THE AUTONOMOUS GIRL"

The Pill liberated women by creating options. They could choose to have sex and avoid pregnancy with almost 100 percent certainty—a historical first. As a result of this new sexual freedom, women were increasingly released from society's double standard, which turned a blind eye to men, but not to women, who engaged in sex before marriage. Like men, many young women began to embrace the idea of having sex purely for pleasure and chose to delay marriage. Women's views on motherhood and careers began to change too. Many more women began to pursue advanced degrees and careers outside the home. Gloria Steinem, a journalist and leading feminist, wrote an article for *Esquire*, a men's magazine, in 1962 about the sexual practices of female college students. Although many of the students she interviewed were already sexually active, Steinem remarked that the Pill's reliability would vanquish the "last remnants of fear of social consequences" from loss of virginity and pregnancy and would "speed American women, especially single women, toward the view that their sex practices are none of society's business." The Pill, she wrote, ushered in the "'autonomous girl'

Gloria Steinem *(seated by wall)* spoke publicly in support of the Pill and the freedom it afforded women. Steinem went on to launch *Ms.*, a feminist magazine, in 1972. Here, she holds a meeting with *Ms.* founding editors Letty Cottin Pogrebin *(standing)* and Patricia Carbine *(seated on floor)*, and other staff.

[who] expects to find her identity neither totally without men nor totally through them. . . . Like men, they are free to take sex, education, work and even marriage when and how they like."

THE SEXUAL REVOLUTION

Not everyone was happy about the Pill. Many Americans feared the era's sexual revolution, a social movement that was overturning traditional views of sex and sexuality and allowing for more personal freedoms. The sexual revolution took place in an era of great social changes in the United States. While women's professional and sexual opportunities were expanding, African Americans were fighting for their civil rights, and many gays and lesbians were openly declaring their sexual orientation. Meanwhile, the nation was involved in the controversial Vietnam War (1957–1975). The public was also rocked by the assassinations of US president John F. Kennedy (1963), his brother Robert F. Kennedy (1968), and the civil rights leader Martin Luther King Jr. (1968).

Many Americans welcomed the social changes of the 1960s, while others feared the reversal of long-held family roles and values. Traditionalists worried that sexual liberation would bring about sexual promiscuity, particularly among young women, and lead to the breakdown of the family. A *U.S. News & World Report* article summed up these concerns. "[Americans are asking] these questions: With birth control so easy and effective, is the last vestige of sexual restraint to go out the window? Will mating be casual and random—as among the animals?"

The Catholic Church vehemently opposed the Pill. John Rock, himself a devout Catholic, tried to convince the Vatican (the governing body of the Catholic Church) that the Pill worked in the same natural way as the rhythm method approved by the church at that time. The Pill, he argued, contained the same hormones found in every woman's reproductive system. To Rock, the only effect the Pill had on a woman's natural menstrual cycle was to increase the length of time during which a woman would be unable to ovulate and therefore remain infertile.

In 1968 Pope Paul VI issued an encyclical known as *Humanae Vitae* (of human life), in which he officially prohibited Catholics from using all artificial methods of contraception, including the Pill. Many Catholic women ignored the encyclical. In fact, a 1970 survey found that approximately 28 percent of Catholic women had used the Pill for contraception despite the church's official ban.

Meanwhile, some members of Congress proclaimed the Pill to be the best way to reduce the nation's large numbers of black children born outside of wedlock and living in poverty.

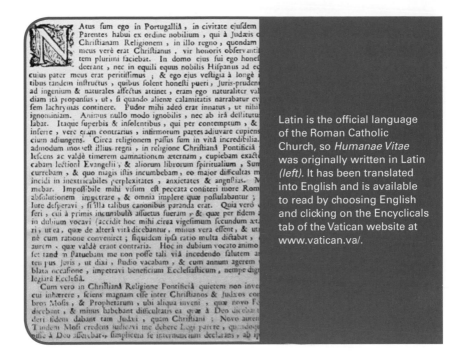

Latin is the official language of the Roman Catholic Church, so *Humanae Vitae* was originally written in Latin *(left)*. It has been translated into English and is available to read by choosing English and clicking on the Encyclicals tab of the Vatican website at www.vatican.va/.

These leaders viewed the Pill as a way to limit fertility in an effort to control population growth. Many black activists responded by denouncing the Pill as an instrument of "race suicide." As one journalist wrote in *Ebony,* a magazine by and for black Americans, "For years, [whites] told us where to sit, where to eat, and where to live. Now they want to dictate our bedroom habits. . . . Now that we've got a little taste of power, white folks want us to call a moratorium on [end to] having children."

GRISWOLD V. CONNECTICUT

With the Pill, Comstock laws were ripe for legal challenge. Estelle Griswold, executive director of the Planned Parenthood League of Connecticut (PPLC), and C. Lee Buxton, its medical director, decided to take a stand. They opened a birth control clinic in Connecticut, where the use of all contraceptives was

Estelle Griswold *(left)* and Mrs. Ernest Jahncke *(right)*, president of the Planned Parenthood League of Connecticut, read a June 1965 Connecticut newspaper headline confirming their victory in *Griswold v. Connecticut*. In this Supreme Court case, the court ruled that a married couple could use contraceptives without interference by the government. With another Supreme Court decision seven years later, birth control would become legal to all adults throughout the United States.

illegal. Shortly after, on November 1, 1961, they were convicted of assisting women in breaking the law by providing contraceptive information, physical examinations, and prescriptions for contraceptive devices to married women.

Griswold and Buxton appealed, and the case went all the way to the US Supreme Court. In the landmark case *Griswold v. Connecticut*, the court ruled in 1965 that the Connecticut law was unconstitutional. The court held that the law "operates directly on an intimate relation of husband and wife" that is within "the zones of privacy" protected by the Constitution's Bill of Rights. A married couple, the court stated, could use contraceptives within the privacy of their relationship without interference by the government. Seven years later, in *Eisenstadt v. Baird*, the US Supreme Court extended the same contraceptive rights to unmarried couples. With the *Griswold* and *Eisenstadt* rulings, contraception was legalized throughout the United States. For most Americans, gone were the days of treating contraceptives as immoral and illegal.

CHAPTER 6
ROE V. WADE

In the climate of rapidly and radically changing attitudes toward sex, reproduction, and gender roles in the United States, abortion again became a center of debate. Advocates of population control were among the strongest voices in favor of lifting state abortion bans. Physicians too supported abortion on the grounds of medical safety, reversing a century of opposition. The medical establishment collected data that demonstrated the safety of physician-administered abortions in the early stages of pregnancy. Safety was a critical issue, since thousands of women—ten thousand in New York City in 1964 alone—were being treated in public, tax-funded hospitals for complications stemming from illegal abortions.

Jazz singer Dee Dee Bridgewater described her abortion experience in 1968: "I had a girlfriend who had a friend who was a nurse and she said that she would give me the abortion. I had to meet her in a hotel room. . . . I was very humiliated. . . . She took out a long rubber hose. . . . She made me lie down on the bed and she inserted this hose, and she said you are going to have to keep this hose in your body for the next couple of days. And two days later I remember starting to hemorrhage. I had to be rushed to emergency. I just remember the excruciating pain."

In response to the large number of dangerous abortions, Protestant clergy formed the Clergy Consultation Service, which helped women have safe abortions in the 1960s.

Meanwhile, a Chicago group called Jane referred women to safe abortion providers and trained members to perform abortions in private homes. The California-based Society for Humane Abortions (formed in 1961) advertised private sessions at homes to teach self-abortion techniques. Yet many women remained desperate.

At that time, wealthier women could convince their doctors to recommend therapeutic abortions. They also could travel to states where enforcement of antiabortion laws was loose or where laws were less restrictive. Or they could go to other countries, such as Japan, where abortions became legal in the 1940s. Recognizing that poor women did not have these options, the American Law Institute—a group of judges, lawyers, and legal scholars—called for reform in 1962. Between 1967 and 1970, thirteen states reformed their laws, legalizing therapeutic abortions. Four states repealed laws and permitted abortions when a woman and her doctor viewed the procedure as necessary.

Severe birth defects among babies in England whose mothers had taken an antinausea drug called thalidomide made headline news in the 1960s. The defects led many Americans to consider quality of human life as part of the conversation about reproduction. Meanwhile, a US outbreak of German measles, which could cause pregnant women to have deformed babies, added to those concerns. As historian James C. Mohr noted, "Abortion no longer seemed to involve a choice between absolutes—life or not life—but matters of degree—what kind of life under what kind of conditions."

Many black leaders, such as the Reverend Jesse Jackson (a civil rights activist), Shirley Chisholm (the first black woman in Congress), and Frances Beal (cofounder of the Black Women's Liberation Committee), wrestled with the conflicts between

Shirley Chisholm became the first black American to serve in Congress, representing New York's Twelfth Congressional District from 1969 to 1983. She is photographed here in her Brooklyn office in 1974, two years after becoming the first woman to run for the Democratic presidential nomination.

reproductive freedom and black freedom. They worried that abortion would be a tool for government and population-control advocates to restrict the reproduction rights of black women. Chisholm and Beal weighed in on the side of legalization of abortion. At first, Jackson was against abortion, but he changed his position when he ran for US president in 1988.

Feminist leaders had begun to connect women's equality with the "right to control their own bodies and lives; to have their voices and decisions treated with respect, and to participate as equals in private and public life." Women organized public forums where they spoke about their own dangerous abortions. They also began to talk of childbearing as a human right. Speaking at a conference on abortion in Chicago in February 1969, Betty Friedan, a leading feminist and the first president of the National Organization for Women (a group formed to end discrimination against women in employment), stated, "The right of a woman to control her reproductive process must be established as a basic and valuable human civil right not to be denied or abridged by the state (government)." The conference announced the formation of the National Association for the Repeal of Abortion Laws (now known as NARAL Pro-Choice America), which advocated decriminalizing abortion. Men too, including cofounder Lawrence Lader, a leading abortion reformer, joined the ranks of NARAL. As legal scholars Linda Greenhouse and Reva Siegel note, feminist lawyers claimed that all women, whether single or married, rich or poor, "should be free to have children, or, not to have children." Having unwanted children forced women to put off other life goals, such as pursing an education or a career or even supporting and feeding the family they already had. Why, they asked, should women be forced to be pregnant?

HOLDING FIRM

While Protestant and Jewish groups mainly supported abortion reform, the Catholic Church was a leading force against abortion. By the late 1960s, the church had become politically involved. For example, when the New York State Legislature considered passing abortion reform in 1967, Catholic priests in seventeen hundred New York churches read a letter declaring that the sanctity of human life "comes from God Himself." That year the National Conference of Catholic Bishops (NCCB) organized and funded the National Right to Life Committee, which spurred local support for the fight against abortion.

The church increasingly promoted its position with nonreligious arguments and legal documents. Church leaders pointed to the US Declaration of Independence, which states that all men are "endowed by their Creator with certain unalienable rights, that among these are life . . ." To end what they viewed as prejudice against the unborn, Americans United for Life (AUL)—a group for all faiths formed by prominent Catholics in 1971—compared abortion to discrimination against African Americans. An essay in the AUL's publication, *Abortion and Social Justice*, asked the following questions: "Would those [people] who argue that abortion is a private matter argue that the exercise of civil rights is purely a private matter between the Black man and the man that [oppresses] them? Certainly not. . . . Abortion is nothing less than a question of civil *rights*: Does the unborn child have a civil right to life? If he or she does, is it not then the duty of *all* citizens . . . regardless of religious faith or private moral sensitivities, to protect the unborn child's civil rights?"

Individual women who favored restrictions on abortions spoke publicly about their own decisions to remain pregnant and give birth. A mother of five testified before a committee of the New Jersey Assembly in 1970. She told of her doctor advising a therapeutic abortion when she became pregnant with her sixth child because of her medical history. In explaining her choice to remain pregnant, she stated, "I realized that even if no one else considered an abortion wrong, that I did and I have to live with me. . . . I beg you to re-direct your time, efforts and monies . . . at the problems that create the need for abortion . . . ignorance, poverty, and especially prejudice. Let's pour our resources into the research of a foolproof contraceptive, into mental-health clinics, into widespread sex education."

By the early 1970s, those against abortion had successfully linked the practice to a decline of moral values in society. One of the most prominent antiabortion voices was Phyllis Schlafly, a Catholic activist who spoke against the changing roles of women. When the US Congress passed the Equal Rights Amendment (ERA) in 1972, promising equal legal protections for women, Schlafly organized STOP (Stop Taking Our Privileges) ERA. Schlafly spoke in bold terms. For example, in a February 1972 newsletter, she warned that the ERA would liberalize abortion and force women to give up their roles as mothers: "Women's libbers are trying to make wives and mothers unhappy with their career, make them feel that they are 'second-class citizens' and 'abject slaves.' Women's libbers are promoting free

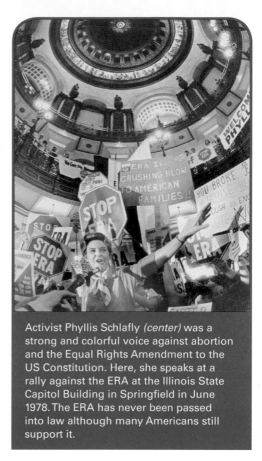

Activist Phyllis Schlafly *(center)* was a strong and colorful voice against abortion and the Equal Rights Amendment to the US Constitution. Here, she speaks at a rally against the ERA at the Illinois State Capitol Building in Springfield in June 1978. The ERA has never been passed into law although many Americans still support it.

sex. . . . They are promoting abortions instead of families. . . . Most women would rather cuddle a baby than a typewriter or factory machine." Her state-by-state appeal to traditional and politically conservative women eventually halted full ratification of the ERA in the late 1970s.

LEGALIZING ABORTION

The battle over abortion had intensified by 1970. That year two young lawyers, Sarah Weddington and Linda Coffee, teamed up to represent Norma McCorvey, a pregnant woman in Texas who wanted an abortion. Little did Weddington and Coffee know that their fight for legal abortion would take them all the way to the US Supreme Court. There they argued one of the most important cases the court has ever decided: *Roe v. Wade*.

Weddington had been practicing law in Austin, Texas, for only two years when a student she knew from the University of Texas approached her at a yard sale in November 1969 to ask for legal advice. A group of students had been working quietly with the Clergy Consultation Service to provide women with referrals to safe abortion providers. But, as the student explained, they were afraid because abortions were illegal in Texas, except when necessary to save a woman's life. Both providers of abortion and accomplices (anyone who "furnished the means" for an abortion) could be fined and imprisoned. And if a woman died from the procedure, the providers and accomplices would be charged with murder. The students wanted to know, Could they be arrested as accomplices if their referral service became more widely known?

Weddington herself had become pregnant in 1967 while she was still attending law school at the University of Texas. With a year left of school, Weddington knew it was the wrong time to have a baby. She remembered her fears. What if the abortion provider was unskilled and the facility was dirty? What if she were arrested? Weddington could afford to pay for a procedure, and the abortion went smoothly. She sympathized with the referral service's concerns.

Meanwhile, state and federal courts were hearing more challenges to abortion statutes. Weddington's legal research led her to consider bringing a case in federal court on the grounds that the Texas statute violated the US Constitution.

Lacking experience in federal court, Weddington turned for help to her law school classmate Coffee, who had worked as a law clerk for a federal judge in Texas. Coffee suggested that they search for a plaintiff (the person bringing the lawsuit) who was directly impacted by the statute: a pregnant woman who wanted an abortion, couldn't afford to travel to obtain a safe and legal abortion, and would be forced to have the baby. With this type of plaintiff, the two women also would be able to file a class action lawsuit (a lawsuit representing everyone with a similar claim). They would be representing the entire class of pregnant women seeking abortions.

MEET JANE ROE

At a Dallas pizza parlor in February 1970, Coffee and Weddington met McCorvey, who was pregnant. Although the lawyers thought that this was McCorvey's second pregnancy, McCorvey later wrote that she had previously had two babies and given both up for adoption. The first time she had gotten pregnant, she was only sixteen. Learning the news, her husband beat her. She ran away to live with her mother, who tricked her into signing adoption papers that named her mother the baby's legal guardian. By the time McCorvey became pregnant a second time, she was abusing drugs and alcohol, barhopping, and engaging in promiscuous

Norma McCorvey is the real person behind the fictitious Jane Roe. McCorvey's wish to end a pregnancy through an abortion became the basis for the landmark Supreme Court case *Roe v. Wade* (1973) affirming a woman's right to an abortion. McCorvey is pictured here on the job as a house painter in January 1983.

sexual encounters. Adoption, she felt, was the best solution in that situation.

With this third pregnancy, McCorvey asked her doctor for an abortion or to refer her somewhere for a safe procedure. When he refused, she thought about traveling to another state where abortion was legal or to Mexico for an illegal abortion. But McCorvey couldn't afford either trip. Next, she visited an adoption lawyer. When McCorvey explained that her first choice was to have an abortion, he too refused to help. Instead, he suggested that she talk to Coffee. He knew that she was searching for a plaintiff in McCorvey's exact situation.

As she sat at the table across from Weddington and Coffee in Dallas, McCorvey explained why she wanted an abortion and how powerless she felt. After listening to Weddington and Coffee describe how their lawsuit might help other women, McCorvey agreed to become the plaintiff. Because McCorvey was worried about publicity, the lawyers listed McCorvey's name on the court papers as Jane Roe. Henry Wade, the Dallas County district attorney responsible for enforcement of the abortion laws in that county, was the defendant (the individual being sued).

The case was argued before the Supreme Court in December 1971 and October 1972. In January 1973, the court issued its momentous decision in *Roe v. Wade*. Building on the right of privacy underlying *Griswold* and *Eisenstadt*, the court held that this right was "broad enough to encompass a woman's decision whether or not to terminate her pregnancy. . . . Maternity, or additional offspring, may force upon the woman a distressful life and future." The court went on to say that during the first three months of pregnancy (the first trimester), a woman's right to have an abortion was absolute.

But the court also ruled that state governments could pass regulations to protect maternal health. The government could also forbid abortion during the last three months of pregnancy (the third trimester), when a fetus is capable of living outside the womb, except when necessary to protect the life or health of the mother.

On the same day the court decided *Roe*, it also ruled on a second case, *Doe v. Bolton*. This case challenged a more lenient Georgia statute that permitted abortion when a woman's life or health was in danger. In *Doe* the court expanded the meaning of a woman's health to include a woman's mental, emotional, and psychological well-being.

When the *Roe v. Wade* decision was announced, Weddington was elated. She later wrote, "The Court's decision was an opportunity for all women. The battle was never 'for abortion'—abortion was not what we wanted to encourage. The battle was for the basic right of women to make their own decisions. There was a basic question underlying the specific issue of abortion: Who is to control and define the lives of women? And our answer was: Not the government!"

CHAPTER 7
THE POLITICS OF ABORTION

In April 1973, just three months after the court decided *Roe v. Wade*, a woman from Massachusetts named Anne (whose last name is confidential) faced a difficult situation. She was four months pregnant. Her husband, claiming he had fallen in love with someone else, had just left her. On her doctor's recommendation, Anne visited a social worker to help work through her concerns. The social worker told Anne that she could have a legal abortion, but Anne said no. She wanted the baby, and her husband's leaving didn't affect that wish. "But that conversation with the social worker," she later explained, "and the knowledge that an abortion would have been legally available had I felt unable to proceed with the pregnancy, added depth and resonance to my desire. This was a most wanted child. I had the choice, and I chose to have a baby."

Anne and many other women chose not to have an abortion in 1973. But that year, 616,000 women did choose to have legal abortions. In reaction, the antiabortion movement in the United States picked up speed within a year of *Roe v. Wade*. Political organizing took place among religious groups that firmly believed in "the traditional social roles of the family, the churches, and the schools" in American life. The Pro-Life Legal Affairs Committee and the National Right to Life Committee, both outgrowths of the NCCB, combined forces with evangelical Protestants and were among the most powerful groups.

These supporters—known as fundamentalists for their literal interpretation of biblical texts and the view that abortion at any stage is murder—joined the Republican Party in large numbers. They advocated for a Human Life Amendment in 1974 to codify their view that life begins at conception. By 1980 the Republican Party had adopted a "constitutional amendment to restore protection of the right to life for unborn children" as part of the party platform. Democrats, on the other hand, supported a woman's "right to choose whether

Antiabortion demonstrators march outside the US Courthouse in downtown Saint Louis, Missouri, in the early 1970s. Abortion deeply divided Americans, even after *Roe v. Wade* established a woman's right to the procedure. Activists have continued to protest and have been successful in leading lawmakers to create limits on where and under what conditions women may seek an abortion.

and when to have a child" and opposed "any constitutional amendment to restrict or overturn" *Roe v. Wade.*

Pro-choice advocates recognized that having an abortion was a morally difficult decision for most women. But they placed a stronger value on the emotional and physical health of a woman than on the potential life of a fetus, particularly before viability (the twenty-fourth week of pregnancy, after which a fetus can survive outside the womb). In this context of deep division over abortion, Ronald Reagan, the Republican presidential candidate in 1980, used the antiabortion message as part of his strategy to win election. He ushered in a presidency where abortion played a major role in politics.

CHALLENGES TO *ROE V. WADE*

In the years and decades that followed Reagan's election, antiabortion forces scored several significant legal and legislative victories. Key decisions included these:

- The Hyde Amendment. Passed by Congress in 1976, this law banned Medicaid funding (federal health coverage for the poor) for abortions for low-income women. The US Supreme Court upheld the ban in *Harris v. McRae* (1980). In subsequent years, Congress expanded the ban to cover abortions for all federal employees, including those in the military.
- *Webster v. Reproductive Health Services.* In this case, the US Supreme Court ruled in 1989 that a state could ban abortions at state-run hospitals, unless an abortion was necessary to save a woman's life.

In 1992 the US Supreme Court ruled in *Planned Parenthood v. Casey* that a state could enact laws that restrict abortion in

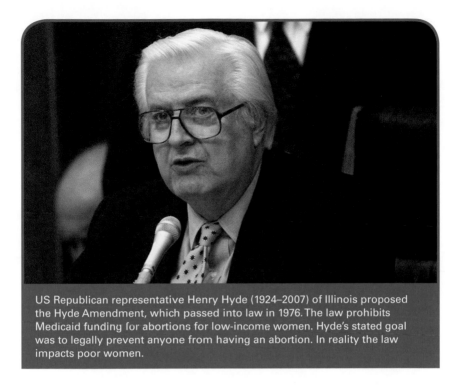

US Republican representative Henry Hyde (1924–2007) of Illinois proposed the Hyde Amendment, which passed into law in 1976. The law prohibits Medicaid funding for abortions for low-income women. Hyde's stated goal was to legally prevent anyone from having an abortion. In reality the law impacts poor women.

the early stages of pregnancy, before viability. In addition, unlike *Roe*, these laws could be enacted for purposes other than protecting a woman's health. They included requirements of pre-abortion counseling, twenty-four-hour waiting periods between first meeting an abortion provider and having the procedure, and parental consent for minors. The court permitted these restrictions as long as they did not create an "undue burden" on women or place "a substantial obstacle" in the way of obtaining an abortion.

Other significant legal decisions and laws in the early twenty-first century included the following:

- *Stenberg v. Carhart* (2000). The US Supreme Court struck down a Nebraska ban on dilation and extraction

(D&X) abortions because the law did not provide an exception for a mother's health. D&X abortions—which the National Right to Life Committee began to refer to as partial-birth abortions—mostly take place in the late second trimester and involve a doctor dilating a woman's cervix to extract the fetus from the womb.

- Partial Birth Abortion Act of 2003. This act was signed into law by President George W. Bush. It banned D&X abortion procedures at all stages of pregnancy, with no exception for a woman's health.
- *Gonzales v. Carhart* (2007). The US Supreme Court rejected a pro-choice challenge to the Partial Birth Abortion Act. For the first time ever, the court permitted an abortion restriction without an exception for a mother's health.

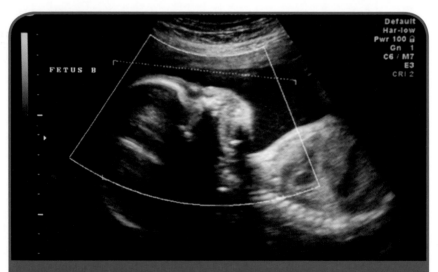

This ultrasound shows one of two twin fetuses in the second trimester. In the twenty-first century, courts are upholding regulations that require abortion providers to show a pregnant woman an ultrasound of the fetus she is seeking to abort.

- *Texas Medical Providers Performing Abortion Services v. Lakey* (2012). The US Court of Appeals for the Fifth Circuit upheld a Texas law requiring that abortion providers show women ultrasound images of their fetuses prior to an abortion. The law also requires providers to play the sound of the fetal heartbeat at high volume so a pregnant woman can hear it. However, in December 2014 the US Court of Appeals for the Fourth Circuit struck down a similar law in North Carolina in *Stuart v. Camnitz.* The US Supreme Court declined to review the case in June 2015, so the decision is binding in North Carolina and other states within the Fourth Circuit.

Many of the antiabortion victories were partially due to a change in the makeup of the nine-member US Supreme Court since the *Roe v. Wade* decision. For example, Justice Sandra Day O'Connor, a moderate judge, retired in 2005, before the *Gonzales v. Carhart* decision. Justice Samuel Alito Jr., her replacement, has been firmly opposed to all forms of abortion at any stage. Alito's vote, along with those of four other conservative justices on the court (Chief Justice John G. Roberts Jr. and Justices Anthony M. Kennedy, Antonin Scalia, and Clarence Thomas), tipped the balance in favor of upholding the ban on the D&X procedure. State and federal courts have also upheld abortion restrictions in regions of the country where more conservative judges have been appointed or elected.

THE LAY OF THE LAND

By 2015 the Supreme Court's decision in *Planned Parenthood v. Casey* opened the door for states in more conservative regions of the country to pass a patchwork of hundreds of abortion restrictions on early-term pregnancies. States in the Midwest and South have passed more antiabortion laws than states in the Northeast and West. Pro-choice advocates continually challenge these new laws in the courts, charging that they place unnecessary barriers, including feelings of shame, in the way of women exercising their constitutional right to an abortion.

Pro-life supporters say that these restrictions, as well as growing support for life of the unborn among young people,

The Insurance Debate

Emergency contraception is a way to prevent pregnancy after unprotected sex. So-called morning-after pills primarily halt ovulation, so the sperm have no egg to fertilize. A health-care provider can also insert a copper IUD after a woman has had unprotected sex as another way to prevent pregnancy. The IUD affects sperm motility (movement) so they can't join with and fertilize an egg.

In 2014 various groups challenged the Patient Protection and Affordable Care Act of 2010 (ACA), a national law that expands health-care coverage and for some people increases the affordability of insurance. The ACA requires employers to provide insurance to their employees to pay for contraception (but not for abortion). Some religious groups, colleges, and universities object to this requirement because they think that emergency contraception induces abortion. They believe that the ACA encroaches on their religious freedom under the Religious Freedom Restoration Act (RFRA) of 1993, which applies at the federal level.

In one case, *Burwell v. Hobby Lobby Stores, Inc.* (June 2014), owners of the Hobby Lobby chain of crafting supply have caused a decline in the number of abortions between 2008 and 2011. Based on two Guttmacher Institute surveys in 2014, though, researchers attributed the declining rates to increased availability, acceptance, and use of newer, long-acting and reversible contraception (LARC) methods. These include IUDs and hormonal implants. Researchers also say that if the rates indicated a growing pro-life trend, they would have seen an increase in the national birthrate. But instead, the birthrate declined significantly (by 9 percent), indicating that births were not replacing abortions.

stores objected to providing health coverage for types of contraception that they likened to abortion. They based their objection on their Christian beliefs that life begins at conception. In a 5–4 decision, the US Supreme Court ruled that a family-owned business such as Hobby Lobby did not have to pay for morning-after contraception. The four justices who dissented pointed out that such businesses could include very large companies with tens of thousands of employees.

In the spring of 2015, Indiana became the first state to adopt a state version of the RFRA. Sixteen state legislatures have introduced state versions of the federal act since then. This trend may lead to other private businesses restricting the types of contraception for which they will provide insurance coverage.

Currently, twenty states permit employers, hospitals, and organizations that oppose contraception for religious reasons to refuse to cover contraception costs in their health-care plans. Six states permit individual pharmacists to refuse to provide any form of contraception, and three states permit pharmacies to refuse to provide emergency contraception.

INFORMED DECISIONS

The antiabortion laws fall into two main categories: those designed to persuade women not to have an abortion and those designed to force the closing of abortion clinics. Many courts have issued opinions on these laws, but the decisions have been inconsistent. Until the US Supreme Court rules on them, they are not binding in all states.

In the first category are laws passed in many states to ensure that women receive sufficient information to voluntarily make an informed decision about undergoing an abortion procedure. For example, thirty-eight states require some sort of parental notification, and/or consent by one or both parents, or approval by a court, for abortions for minors. Twenty-six states enforce a waiting period (usually twenty-four hours) between a woman's first appointment for abortion counseling and the abortion procedure. Some states require a waiting period of forty-eight or seventy-two hours, excluding holidays and weekends. Proponents of these laws claim that women must be given time to evaluate their choices to make an informed decision. But pro-choice advocates contend that women are capable of making their own choices without enforced waiting periods and that these laws are veiled attempts to restrict women's access to abortion.

In many states, the medical information provided to women about the procedure is inaccurate or misleading. For example, in seven states, abortion providers are required to counsel women about the serious mental health consequences they may suffer if they proceed with an abortion. Having an abortion can be a wrenching decision for a woman and her family, regardless of her position on the legality of the procedure. Yet the American Psychiatric Association (APA) has found that women who have abortions are no more likely to suffer long-term effects of depression than are those giving birth from an unwanted pregnancy.

In addition, several states direct health providers to counsel—inaccurately—that abortion increases a woman's risk for breast cancer or will lead to future infertility problems. For example, despite a scientific study conducted by the National Cancer Institute ruling out a link between abortion and breast cancer, Texas facilities continue to provide written materials declaring that the evidence is inconclusive. And although US surgeon general C. Everett Koop ruled out physical repercussions from abortion as early as 1989, four states still inaccurately counsel a risk of future infertility.

Other mandated counseling laws aim to compel women to consider the implications of destroying potential life. Twenty-three states require a woman to view an ultrasound of the fetus before undergoing an abortion, even though it is medically unnecessary. Some states go even further by requiring that providers describe the image of the fetus to the pregnant woman. In five states, providers are directed to inform women that personhood begins at conception. Physicians in twelve states are also required to tell women that fetuses feel pain during an abortion.

Overall, pro-choice advocates argue that these types of requirements violate the privacy and trust necessary to a doctor–patient relationship. Pro-choice advocates stress that the requirements force doctors to follow a script containing false information and to perform ultrasounds that are medically unnecessary. No other medical procedures are regulated by the state in such a manner. Speaking on a panel at Yale University, Dr. Nancy Stanwood, board chair of

Do Abortions Cause Fetal Pain?

Activists in the antiabortion movement believe that a fetus can feel pain. They say that pain is evidence of a human life that should not be destroyed, even before viability. Mary Spaulding Balch, the state policy director of the Right to Life Committee, says that when a "member of the human family has reached a point where they are capable of feeling pain," all abortions should be prohibited.

Medical science does not support fetal pain theories prior to viability. For a fetus to feel pain, most neuroscientists think that the brain's cortex first must be developed, which occurs around the twenty-third week of pregnancy. Then the neural passageways must be able to transmit the sensory data, which begins to occur around the twenty-sixth week or later. The limited available evidence suggests that fetuses begin to feel pain during the third trimester, around twenty-seven weeks of pregnancy. The American Congress of Obstetricians and Gynecologists and the Royal College of Obstetricians and Gynaecologists in England endorse this theory. Other neuroscientists, though, think that pain can be felt before development of the cortex. They say that development of the thalamus, which occurs at around twenty weeks, is the key to feeling pain.

Physicians for Reproductive Health (PRH), a national advocacy group for physicians, summarized this position: "My watchword (to the states) is please, get out of our exam rooms. We are professionals, we are well-trained, and we really want to adhere to the best science and the best ethics of our profession."

TRAP LAWS

In the second category, the antiabortion movement has been

Ten states currently have laws banning abortion at twenty-two weeks after a woman's last period (or twenty weeks after fertilization)—before viability—on the grounds of fetal pain. Pro-choice advocates challenge the position that fetal pain is a valid reason for restricting abortions before viability. Thus far, courts have agreed. For example, in *Isaacson v. Horne*, a lawsuit brought by three physicians who practice abortion, the US Court of Appeals for the Ninth Circuit struck down an Arizona law outlawing abortion after the twentieth week of pregnancy. The court relied on the decision in *Roe v. Wade* that a woman may not be deprived of her constitutional right to an abortion before viability. The ruling in *Isaacson* is binding in the Ninth Circuit, an area that covers several western states, and the US Supreme Court has declined to review the case.

In May 2015, though, the US House of Representatives passed a ban on abortions after twenty weeks. Called the Pain-Capable Unborn Child Protection Act, the bill states that "there is substantial medical evidence that an unborn child is capable of experiencing pain at least by 20 weeks after fertilization, if not earlier." If the bill passes the Senate, President Barack Obama has said he will refuse to sign it into law.

successful in pushing for state laws that restrict abortion clinics so much that many are forced to close. Known as Targeted Regulation of Abortion Provider (TRAP) laws, these laws vary from state to state. Almost all TRAP laws in the twenty-four states that have them require abortion clinics to follow standards set for clinics that provide significantly more difficult and risky same-day surgeries. For example, twelve states require a specific size for rooms where abortions are performed and for the width of clinic hallways.

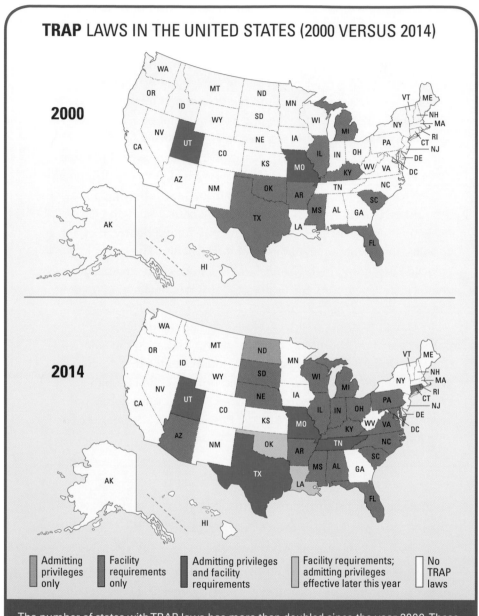

TRAP LAWS IN THE UNITED STATES (2000 VERSUS 2014)

2000

2014

Admitting privileges only

Facility requirements only

Admitting privileges and facility requirements

Facility requirements; admitting privileges effective later this year

No TRAP laws

The number of states with TRAP laws has more than doubled since the year 2000. These maps based on Guttmacher Institute data lay out the differing requirements in various states in the years 2000 (*top*) and 2014 (*bottom*).

Pro-choice advocates argue that some of the restrictions are unrelated to clinic safety, such as laws specifying the number of parking spaces a clinic must have or the size of janitorial closets. Sixteen states mandate these requirements even for clinics where medication (nonsurgical) rather than surgical abortions are provided. Many clinics close because upgrade expenses are too high.

Other TRAP laws require physicians who practice abortions to have admitting privileges (the right to practice) at a local hospital in case of a patient emergency requiring hospitalization. Pro-choice advocates claim these restrictions are unfair. No similar laws restrict physicians who practice any other specialty of medicine. The laws are impractical as well, since many women live far from abortion clinics, which are increasingly rare. A pregnant woman who needs hospitalization will likely seek help near her home, not at a hospital near an abortion clinic. In addition, hospitals typically grant admitting privileges to only those doctors who can guarantee they will treat a certain number of patients at that hospital. Since patients rarely need hospitalization after abortions, doctors who perform abortions often can't guarantee the number of patients an admitting hospital requires.

Antiabortion forces claim that this mandate is meant to ensure that a woman can receive emergency hospital care as a result of an abortion, if necessary. Pro-choice advocates, on the other hand, point to statistics that prove that abortion is safer than most outpatient procedures. Less than 0.03 percent of women (about one out of every three thousand) have complications from abortions. Death rates are very low—four women in one million. In fact, fourteen times more deaths occur during childbirth than as a result of abortions. Also, like all health facilities, government agencies license

Medication Abortions

Women can choose two different ways to have an abortion—either by a surgical procedure or by taking abortion medication. Various surgical options are available depending on the week of pregnancy. The most common method is vacuum aspiration, a procedure used up to sixteen weeks after a woman's last period that suctions the fetus from the uterus.

In 2000 the FDA approved a medication regimen for abortion that consists of two pills. A woman takes the first pill, Mifeprex (the US brand name for mifepristone, also known as RU486), at the clinic. She takes the second pill, misoprostol, at home twenty-four to forty-eight hours after swallowing the first pill. A follow-up visit to the doctor is necessary to make sure the fetus has been completely discharged from the uterus. Women can opt for medication abortions up to nine weeks after the first day of their last period.

Medication abortions are increasingly common in the United States. About 23 percent of women having abortions in nonhospital settings, such as in clinics or at a private doctor's office, opted for abortion pills in 2011, up from 6 percent in 2001. Women say they prefer medication abortions, as they require fewer trips to a clinic and can be administered early in pregnancy. Women who live in rural areas or who must travel long distances

and monitor abortion facilities for safety compliance. And by law, all hospitals are required to admit patients requiring emergency care, no matter the situation.

The practical outcome of the TRAP laws is that hospitals that don't support abortions frequently refuse admitting privileges to abortion providers. And without doctors with admitting privileges, many abortion clinics have shut down. This has left some states with few or no abortion providers. For women in areas where clinics have closed, that often involve taking days off from work and the expense of a hotel stay also prefer that the procedure can be done in the privacy of their home.

Since 2000, states have enacted laws that restrict women's access to medication abortions. For example, in spring 2015, Arizona passed an antiabortion law requiring physicians to inform women, before giving the second pill in the medication abortion regimen, "that it may be possible to reverse" the procedure. In a *New York Times* article, Dr. Ilana Addis, chairwoman of the Arizona section of the American Congress of Obstetricians and Gynecologists, explained, "It [the reversal method] has no data behind it, absolutely no science to show that this is an effective method."

Meanwhile, many abortion rights advocates are looking for ways to enable more women to have access to medication abortions. Rebecca Gomperts, a physician, set up Women on Web, a telemedicine website, to help supply abortion pills to women who live in countries where abortion is illegal.

In the United States, pro-choice activists are proposing over-the-counter sales of misoprostol. They are also supporting the right of doctors to legally write prescriptions for mifepristone that women could fill at pharmacies and administer at home rather than in a clinic.

the nearest abortion clinic may be hundreds of miles away, perhaps even in a different state altogether. Supporters of abortion say that the scarcity of clinics places undue hardship on women seeking a legal abortion. Antiabortion advocates, such as Mississippi governor Phil Bryant, make no bones about the goal of TRAP laws. Bryant said, in signing his state's TRAP law in 2012, "Today you see the first step in a movement to do what we campaigned on . . . to try to end abortion in Mississippi."

As decades of rulings, requirements, and Gallup polls show, Americans are divided about abortion. Debate frequently surrounds what it means to be pro-choice and pro-life. Pro-choice advocates argue for more than just abortion rights. They contend that their main mission is to protect the broad range of needs that together ensure women's health. They support the availability of reproductive health services—including sex education, contraception, prenatal health care, safe childbirth, and abortion—for all women regardless of economic background. They recognize that a fetus is a form of life but do not view it as a potential human being until after it can survive outside the womb, which most doctors agree is around the twenty-fourth week of pregnancy.

Even the most avid pro-choice supporters recognize that abortion should be infrequent. They feel that contraception, not abortion, should be a woman's first line of defense in avoiding pregnancy. Yet, when an abortion is wanted—for any reason—they say that the procedure must remain legal or it will be unsafe. With these beliefs in mind, the pro-choice movement favors sex education programs that include information about contraception and abstaining from sex. Pro-choice activists think that many state laws and court rulings are aimed at unfairly and dangerously limiting women's legal rights to reproductive health care and to the right to choose what is best for their bodies, families, and lives.

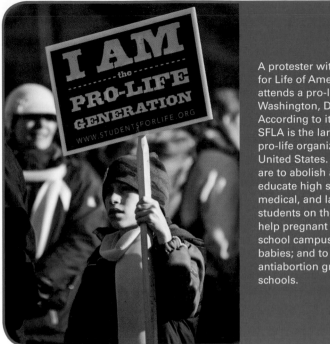

A protester with Students for Life of America (SFLA) attends a pro-life rally in Washington, DC, in 2015. According to its website, SFLA is the largest youth pro-life organization in the United States. SFLA's goals are to abolish abortion; to educate high school, college, medical, and law school students on the issues; to help pregnant women on school campuses keep their babies; and to organize antiabortion groups at their schools.

Pro-life advocates state that their main mission is to protect the right to life of all human beings, including the unborn. They defend all life from the moment of conception to natural death and view abortion as a form of murder. They advocate a personhood amendment to the US Constitution that would establish the right to life of the unborn. For the pro-life movement, a "culture of life" means reserving sex for marriage and procreation. And since many pro-life advocates feel that birth control promotes sex outside of marriage and leads to abortions, they are against contraception for teens and support abstinence–only sex education in schools. They favor fertility technologies that do not destroy fertilized eggs. Pro-life advocates promote legislation and political action to encourage women to remain pregnant and to consider adoption if they cannot keep the baby. They also seek to close clinics that provide abortions.

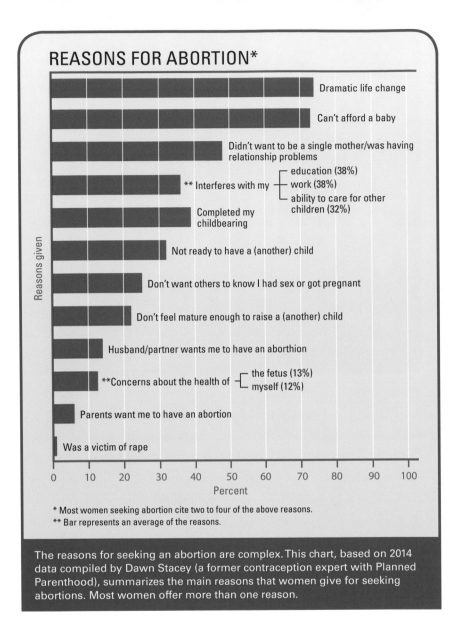

REASONS FOR ABORTION*

Dramatic life change

Can't afford a baby

Didn't want to be a single mother/was having relationship problems

** Interferes with my ── education (38%)
── work (38%)
── ability to care for other children (32%)

Completed my childbearing

Not ready to have a (another) child

Don't want others to know I had sex or got pregnant

Don't feel mature enough to raise a (another) child

Husband/partner wants me to have an aborthion

**Concerns about the health of ── the fetus (13%)
── myself (12%)

Parents want me to have an abortion

Was a victim of rape

Reasons given

Percent — 0 10 20 30 40 50 60 70 80 90 100

* Most women seeking abortion cite two to four of the above reasons.
** Bar represents an average of the reasons.

The reasons for seeking an abortion are complex. This chart, based on 2014 data compiled by Dawn Stacey (a former contraception expert with Planned Parenthood), summarizes the main reasons that women give for seeking abortions. Most women offer more than one reason.

Polls show that most Americans are not entirely pro-choice or pro-life. In 1995 a significant majority of adult Americans (56 percent) viewed themselves as pro-choice, favoring the legal right to abortion. By 2009 more Americans (51 percent) identified themselves as pro-life (against abortion) than pro-choice (42 percent). By 2014 the gap had closed more, with 47 percent of Americans identifying as pro-choice and 46 percent as pro-life. The other 7 percent were undecided. (They didn't know how they felt or refused to answer.)

This data can be misleading, as answers depend on the specific questions polled. For example, in response to a 2013 Gallup survey question of whether or not the US Supreme Court should overturn *Roe v. Wade,* more Americans (53 percent) said no than those who said yes (29 percent). The number of undecided Americans (18 percent) was largely due to a greater number of people in the eighteen to twenty-nine age category who expressed no opinion at all. This trend suggests that this group may not be as familiar with US Supreme Court decisions impacting abortion as are older Americans. Yet, among younger adults who do express an opinion, 54 percent identify themselves as pro-choice and 36 percent as pro-life.

Other factors also influence the issue. For example, among women, 50 percent identify as pro-choice and about 41 percent as pro-life. Men and older Americans (aged fifty-five-plus) lean toward pro-life (about 50 percent) rather than pro-choice (44 percent). Easterners as a group are the most pro-choice Americans (59 percent) versus 35 percent who are pro-life. The Midwest (46 percent pro-choice to 50 percent pro-life) and West (48 percent pro-choice to 47 percent pro-life) are about evenly split. Southerners as a group are more pro-life (49 percent) than pro-choice (41 percent).

Political and religious beliefs, education, and yearly income also affect pro-choice and pro-life positions. Americans who call themselves pro-choice are most likely to be nonreligious, politically liberal or Democrats, have graduate degrees, earn incomes of $75,000 or more each year, and live in the suburbs.

Those people who identify as pro-life are more likely to be Protestants or affiliated with other non-Catholic Christian denominations. (Among Americans who are Catholic, 48 percent are pro-choice and 45 percent are pro-life.) They typically earn less than $30,000 a year and do not have a college education. Pro-life Americans also tend to be Republicans or politically conservative. In February 2015, only 34 percent of Americans claimed "they are satisfied with current US abortion policies," the lowest rate since 2001 to 2008, when at least 40 percent or more expressed satisfaction. This trend reflects a growing number of Republicans who prefer stricter abortion laws.

Much of the uncertainty over abortion lies in how Americans view abortion at different stages of pregnancy. A significant majority, 61 percent of those polled, supports the right to an abortion during the first trimester. Yet 64 percent think abortion should be illegal during the second trimester. In 2014 about 50 percent supported "limited abortion rights," with 28 percent thinking abortion should be legal throughout the third trimester and only 21 percent saying that abortion should be banned entirely.

VIOLENCE

A very small minority of Americans holds extreme views that condone violence to stop abortion at all cost. Over the decades, the violence and intimidation have included eight murders, the bombing of abortion clinics, the stalking and assaulting of abortion clinic workers and their families, death threats, and the blocking of clinic entrances to prevent women seeking abortions from going inside.

Because much of the abortion-related violence and passionate protest take place at entrances to abortion clinics, the

US Congress passed the Freedom of Access to Clinic Entrances (FACE) Act in 1994. The law protects clinic workers and patients from physical injury, harassing phone calls, hate mail, death threats, blockades, or other means that interfere with a woman's right to obtain an abortion. The act also punishes attempts to bomb or otherwise destroy clinics. Sixteen states and the District of Columbia have passed similar laws.

Three states also have buffer zone laws that limit how close protesters can stand to abortion clinic entrances. Typically the buffer zone is about 25 to 35 feet (8 to 11 meters) around the clinic entrance. Other states have declared buffer zones around patients. Protesters cannot violate this space without verbal permission from the patient. The zones allow protesters to legally express their views while also protecting women seeking an abortion from feeling physically threatened or otherwise intimidated.

ONLINE CAMPAIGNS

Some antiabortion activists have turned to the Internet to widen their campaign. In one example, militant antiabortion advocates created a website known as the Nuremberg Files (named for the trials against Nazi war criminals after World War II). The website—claiming to do God's work—encouraged supporters to send in names, addresses, and photos of abortion providers and their family members; clinic owners and workers; and judges, politicians, and law enforcement officials who support abortion rights. The list was coded to indicate whether individuals had been injured or killed. For example, within hours after James Kopp shot and killed abortion provider Dr. Barnett Slepian through his kitchen window in 1998, a line appeared through Slepian's name on the website to indicate his death.

Dr. Willie Parker

Every day, Dr. Willie Parker *(left)* faces the risk of violence to provide abortions. Parker is an obstetrician and gynecologist, a board member of Physicians for Reproductive Health, and has received many awards for his work on behalf of women's reproductive rights. Many of the women he treats at the only remaining abortion clinic in Mississippi travel up to seven hours to see him. "We're fighting to keep this clinic open," Parker says. "I want to make sure that if women can go through all those barriers to get to the care, then there's someone there to provide it. Because it doesn't matter if abortion rights are legal if there's no one there to provide that care."

Parker, a religious Christian from a fundamentalist background, travels a route to abortion clinics in the South that is about the same as the path abortion provider Dr. David Gunn followed before he was shot and killed by antiabortion extremist Michael F. Griffin in 1993. But Parker is unafraid. "My understanding of how important it is for women to have access [to abortion] allows me to ignore the people who strongly disagree with what I do, the people who are somewhat threatening in terms of harassment verbally—I've had my experience with this," he explains.

For Parker, performing abortions—particularly for the many women of color who come to the clinic because they lack access to contraception and other reproductive health services—is a matter of conscience. "When you think something is the right thing to do, you have to follow your conscience and ignore everything else," he says. "No matter what other people say about it, it's always right to help someone in need. . . . I don't feel so courageous as much as I feel like I have an opportunity to do something that I believe in."

The American Coalition of Life Activists (ACLA), which provided information to the website, also promoted a media campaign using Wild West–style wanted posters. The posters offered rewards for the arrest of twelve specific abortion providers. In response, Planned Parenthood of Columbia/Willamette, Oregon, several physicians, and an abortion clinic sued the ACLA. In 2002 the US Court of Appeals for the Ninth Circuit affirmed a jury verdict for the plaintiffs and damages in the amount of $109 million. The court stated that the website and the posters were threats to providers' lives. As such, they did not fall under the protections of the First Amendment right to free speech, and the Nuremberg Files website was ordered to shut down. The US Supreme Court refused to review the case. Since then the website has launched under different names to continue its aggressive collection of information. One recent campaign encourages supporters to e-mail video webcasts of people entering and leaving abortion clinics. The website operators claim to be collecting the information for potential use in any legal proceedings against abortion providers and to intimidate women seeking abortions.

PRO-LIFE TACTICS

How has the antiabortion movement achieved success in certain areas? How are pro-choice advocates responding?

The majority of antiabortion activists are conservative Christians. While they are a minority of American voters (16 percent), they are well funded, united, politically active, and vocal. Large national organizations, such as Americans United for Life, the National Right to Life Committee, and the Alliance Defending Freedom, challenge abortion rights. They publish suggested wording for state legislators to use in crafting laws, and they organize local antiabortion demonstrations. Pro-life church and community leaders encourage voter turnout among their supporters. The Republican Party and the Tea Party platforms oppose abortion. Some Republicans and Tea Party members also oppose contraception and sex education in the public schools. These politicians look to the large national antiabortion organizations for support.

After the 2010 national elections, Republicans and Tea Party politicians captured a majority of the seats in the US House of Representatives. They also gained more seats in the US Senate, increasing their minority position. That year voters elected a large number of conservative state legislators across the nation, empowering states to enact abortion restrictions. The 2012 elections did not significantly alter this political lineup.

The rapid advance of medical technology is also influencing the abortion debate. Advanced sonograms, genetic testing, and technologies that help women with fertility problems become pregnant have shifted the way many Americans understand fetal development. The fetus, even in the early weeks of pregnancy, seems more real to many people than it did back in the days of *Roe v. Wade*. Many Americans, even those who support abortion rights, question at what point the right to life comes into play.

In addition, the antiabortion movement has blurred the line between abortions that occur early in pregnancy and those that occur later in pregnancy, after viability. The vast majority of abortions (89 percent) occur in the first twelve weeks of pregnancy, and one-third occur in the first six weeks. Late-term abortions do occur—usually when a woman's doctor discovers fetal abnormalities, when a woman's health is at risk, or when a doctor determines that a fetus will be born dead. The methods used in later-term abortions are much more invasive than those used earlier in pregnancy. Many Americans are disturbed by such procedures and feel deeply emotional about them. The antiabortion movement has linked these emotions to voting behavior. They encourage voters to turn out to vote for politicians who support outlawing all abortion, even though late-term abortions after viability make up only a very small minority (about 1 percent) of all abortions. These emotional responses have emboldened pro-life legislators to push for measures that slowly chip away at abortion rights.

Professor Helen M. Alvaré, an expert in family law at George Mason University School of Law and an adviser to the US Conference of Catholic Bishops, said, "Because abortion destroys human life at its most vulnerable moment, it is a human rights imperative to seek legal protection for that life, even when a total ban on abortion is unrealistic. The pro-life movement's proudest achievement is our creation of more than 3,000 centers assisting mostly poor women to keep their children and build new lives together. We also seek to ban later-term abortions, because a lot of Americans agree about these. The pro-choice movement uses the size and invisibility of the fetus as a reason to allow abortion, whereas a pro-life stance says the unborn's vulnerability calls for extra protection."

PRO-CHOICE TACTICS

Pro-choice advocates are fighting back with relentless challenges to state laws that limit a woman's ability to exercise her right to an abortion. Stephanie Toti is a senior counsel (attorney) at the Center for Reproductive Rights (CRR), a legal advocacy group based in New York City. She says that it's important to fight the restrictions "so that the debate stays focused on the middle ground." She points out that most Americans aren't pro–abortion rights 100 percent of the time. "People have lots of qualifiers about abortion," she explained. "But the idea is to give an empathetic message. There are times when you or your family member might want one. The question really is do you want it available, if you need it? The goal of the pro-choice movement is to protect women and their families even if individuals say they themselves would never have an abortion." Using this message, CRR has successfully helped block abortion bans, TRAP laws, and barriers to medication abortions in many states.

Pro-choice forces in government are also working on laws to protect abortion rights and other reproductive freedoms. For example, to counter the loss of abortion clinics and providers in California, the state permits licensed physician's assistants, nurses, and midwives to perform abortions. In other states, legislators are working to pass laws that prohibit hospitals from denying admitting privileges to physicians who conduct abortions. On the federal level, Senator Richard Blumenthal, a Democrat from Connecticut, and Representative Judy Chu, a Democrat from California, introduced the Women's Health Protection Act in 2013. The act aims to protect women against state laws that restrict reproductive health and a woman's ability to make her own health-related decisions. So far, 35 senators and 133 representatives have backed the bill, although more votes are needed to pass the bill into law.

Many physicians are also vocally pro-choice. Physicians for Reproductive Health want to "remove the stigma" associated with women who undergo abortion and their providers because of laws advocated by antichoice groups and legislators. PRH also speaks out against laws that are based on politics and ideology rather than on sound reproductive medicine. The group also points out legislation that is harmful to the trusting doctor–patient relationship.

PRH board chairperson Nancy Stanwood calls for "conscience protection" for doctors. She notes that state laws protect nurses and doctors who refuse to perform abortions. PRH calls for similar protections for doctors who provide abortions. For example, PRH believes that doctors who choose to perform abortions shouldn't be denied admitting privileges at hospitals.

Scientists and medical researchers are also part of the picture. Over the last several decades, pharmaceutical companies have introduced new, longer-acting, and more effective contraceptive methods. These patches, IUDs, and morning-after pills, when used properly, help reduce the number of unwanted pregnancies. The availability of medication abortions permits women to have the procedure early on in pregnancy, in the privacy of their own homes, and without the expense of frequent doctor visits. Pro-choice researchers claim that these medical advances, along with comprehensive sex education, will continue to decrease the need for abortion.

Organizations such as Planned Parenthood and NARAL Pro-Choice America lobby state and local government leaders to support abortion rights. The groups also organize rallies and petitions; work to elect pro-choice political candidates; and lobby for women's access to abortion, birth control, and sex education. Since Medicaid and other federal health plans currently do not cover the cost of abortion, these organizations also advocate for government funding for abortions for low-income women. In July 2013, women's reproductive health and rights groups organized with youth advocates.

Reproductive Justice

Reproductive justice began as a movement among women of color in the United States who believed that one of the best ways to fight poverty was to provide minority women with access to birth control. Most reproductive rights and pro-choice organizations in the United States and abroad have since adopted this philosophy. Reproductive justice acknowledges reproductive rights as part of a framework of basic human rights recognized by the US Constitution, as well as by international treaties and United Nations declarations. The United States has ratified three major international human rights treaties that ensure reproductive freedom.

Reproductive justice advocates say that all women, regardless of race, ethnicity, religion, sexual orientation, economic status, or age have certain reproductive rights. This holds true whether they are immigrants, disabled, in prison, or without legal citizenship. These basic claims include a woman's right to make her own decisions about reproduction; her right to information, reproductive health services, and safety during pregnancy and childbirth; and her right to parent and provide care for her children.

Reproductive justice groups also target the economic, social, political, and environmental issues that affect women's reproductive choices. This work includes ensuring that employers provide parental leave after the birth of a child; that communities offer affordable child care programs; that workplaces, homes, and communities are safe and free of air pollution and toxic chemicals; and that comprehensive sex education is available in low-income neighborhoods. Since rates of unintended pregnancy are highest among low-income and minority women, women and men of color greatly feel the effects of unequal access to reproductive justice.

The 8 Categories of Human Rights:

Civil Rights

Economic Rights

Cultural Rights

Political Rights

Representation

Equality

Medical care

Natural resources

Clean Air & Water

Living wage

Freedom of choice

Housing

Social Rights

Environmental Rights

Sexual Rights

Developmental Rights

Celebrate the 64th Year of the Universal Declaration of Human Rights December 10th!

WWW.SISTERSONG.NET

SisterSong has eighty grassroots organizations in the United States representing five primary ethnic populations/indigenous nations: American Indian/Indigenous, Black/African American, Latina/ Puerto Rican, Arab American/ Middle Eastern, and Asian/Pacific Islander, as well as white allies and men. The group launched in 1997 to work for reproductive rights and sexual health for women of color. This poster lists eight categories of human rights that SisterSong feels are critical to ensuring those goals.

They launched a campaign called All*Above All. The goal is to engage women and men aged eighteen to thirty and people of color to fight to repeal the Hyde Amendment and to ensure Medicaid coverage for all aspects of prenatal care, including abortion care.

With both sides of the abortion debate entrenched in their positions, the battle is unlikely to end soon. In the view of historian Ruth Rosen, some of the pushback on abortion rights is still partly due to the societal changes brought on by the Pill. These changes include women's growing sexual and economic freedoms and their increasing visibility in high-power professions, such as law, business, and politics. "Ever since 1973," Rosen comments, "abortion has become a symbol of women's freedom. . . . Their sexual freedom is not new; but [abortion] still symbolizes the fact that men can no longer control [women's] bodies or their choices to have children."

CHAPTER 9
BRAVE NEW WORLD

Medical technologies are exploding in almost all areas, including reproductive medicine. Since the 1990s, people around the world have used assisted reproductive technologies (ART) to give birth to more than three million babies. These new technologies help infertile couples conceive. They also allow single heterosexual men and women, as well as lesbian, gay, bisexual, and transgender (LGBT) singles and couples, to have offspring to which they are genetically related. In the twenty-first century, ART has completely changed what it means to have a baby and to be a parent. For those searching for a way to have a biologically connected family, ART can produce a miracle.

Despite these benefits, this new reproductive frontier has opened the door to legal and ethical concerns. In an interview with *USA Today,* Marcy Darnovsky, executive director of the Center for Genetics and Society, called the United States "the Wild Wild West of the fertility industry." Unlike many other developed nations, the United States generally does not regulate the industry, which is hugely profitable ($3.5 billion a year in the United States). Darnovsky said that US lawmakers shy away from dealing with ART because of the political controversies surrounding abortion, contraception, and medical research. For example, in stem cell research, scientists study embryos to learn how these cells develop and grow into specialized cells, such as skin or liver cells, as part of

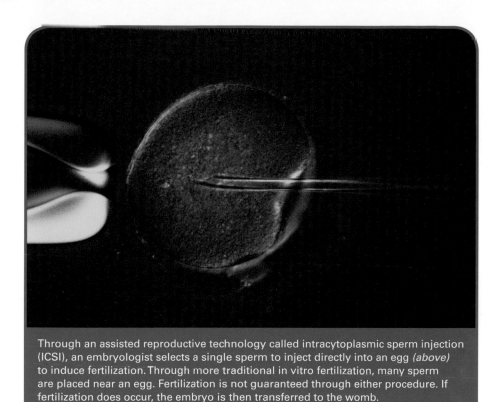

Through an assisted reproductive technology called intracytoplasmic sperm injection (ICSI), an embryologist selects a single sperm to inject directly into an egg *(above)* to induce fertilization. Through more traditional in vitro fertilization, many sperm are placed near an egg. Fertilization is not guaranteed through either procedure. If fertilization does occur, the embryo is then transferred to the womb.

the effort to figure out ways to replace or revitalize damaged or diseased cells in the body. Antiabortion groups are against stem cell research because embryos are destroyed after they are a few days old. But for those who support the research, the potential for curing diseases outweighs the destruction of an embryo, despite its potential for human life.

The one federal law that does exist regarding ART, the Fertility Clinic Success Rate and Certification Act of 1992, mandates licensing of fertility clinics in the United States. The law also requires that clinics report to the Centers for Disease Control and Prevention (CDC) various factors and techniques that contribute to their annual rates of success (the numbers of women delivering live babies). The CDC then lists the statistics on its website so potential ART users can analyze the data in choosing a clinic and deciding on which fertility methods achieve the best results. Clinics are not fined if they do not comply with the law, however.

With little oversight, many fertility specialists do not adequately inform patients of the risks and long-term effects of various procedures. For example, researchers say that more studies are needed to understand the long-term effects of stimulating ovaries and increasing egg production for in vitro fertilization (IVF, a procedure for fertilizing an egg outside the body and then inserting it into a woman's uterus). Because of increased egg production, IVF often leads to twins and other multiple births. A woman carrying more than one fetus faces more health risks during pregnancy and childbirth, as do the babies.

ART is extremely expensive. For example, one cycle of IVF costs between $10,000 and $14,000. Most women require multiple attempts before becoming pregnant, so the costs mount quickly. In some nations of western Europe, the government pays for IVF. In the United States, the government—and most private insurance companies—do not. Reproductive rights advocates say that this is not fair and are working to make IVF and other infertility procedures available to middle and low-income people. In addition, these advocates support the use of ART for the development of all types of families, including LGBT couples.

SEX SELECTION

A particularly controversial reproductive technology associated with IVF—and available since the late 1980s—is preimplantation genetic diagnosis (PGD). In PGD, doctors extract a single cell from an embryo to analyze its deoxyribonucleic acid (DNA). This material contains all genetic information. Most often doctors rely on PGD to screen for serious genetic disorders, in which case parents usually opt not to have the embryo implanted. But parents can also use PGD to choose the sex of the child they will have. (Parents can also use a less reliable and invasive procedure known as sperm sorting, but most choose to use PGD). If PGD reveals an embryo to be the desired sex, it will be implanted in the woman's uterus, hopefully leading to pregnancy. In 2013 about six thousand PGD procedures for sex selection took place in the United States. Each cost about $18,000.

The American Society for Reproductive Medicine (ASRM) is a professional group that counsels fertility specialists on ethical issues. The society takes a stand against the use of PGD for sex selection. But the ASRM has no regulatory power. Fertility clinics advertise sex selection as a way of balancing a family. But the ASRM and others opposed to sex selection believe the procedure devalues females. Most clients who use sex selection choose a boy over a girl. This preference is reflected in national polling. For instance, in a 2011 Gallup poll, 40 percent of Americans said that if they could have only one child, they preferred a boy baby; 28 percent favored a girl, and 26 percent said they didn't care.

Couples who undergo PGD and other ART often fertilize several eggs to have the best chance of an embryo that will support a pregnancy. Antiabortion groups speak out against these procedures because they lead to discarding viable embryos, which they view as a form of life. Many couples donate their unused embryos for stem cell or other medical research. But most people struggle with moral qualms over what to do with those that are left over. Some choose to freeze them for their own future use or donate them to infertile couples. But many embryos are also destroyed or sit unused in scientific laboratories for years. And once couples have a child of their own, their earlier decisions about unused

China's One-Child Policy

In the 1950s, Chinese ruler Mao Zedong encouraged population growth as a way to increase China's economic power and stature in the world. But by 1962, a devastating famine had spread throughout the nation. China's food supply could no longer feed its citizens. Demographers (experts who study population trends) urged population control. Leaders put a one-child-per-family policy into place in 1979. Depending on where a couple lived, the government imposed heavy fines for exceeding the limit. Stories of government-forced abortions and sterilizations also surfaced. By 2009 demographers claimed the policy had prevented the births of about 250 million people.

But critics pointed out that the law encouraged sex discrimination in a country that favors male over female children. Pregnant Chinese women used ultrasounds and other technologies to determine the sex of fetuses and then aborted those that were female. They also abandoned or killed girls at

embryos may waver. For example, they might be uncomfortable with the idea of donating an embryo to a couple in need when that embryo, if it succeeds in supporting a pregnancy to birth, would be a sibling to their own child.

Those in favor of choosing a baby's sex argue that parents have a right to sex selection in much the same way they have a right to choose when and whether to have a child. Others disagree, claiming that choosing a child's sex will open the door to "designer babies," eugenics, and controlling the genetic makeup of future generations. The ability to select traits such as eye color, skin color, and intelligence—choosing among perceived "good versus bad" traits—may also lead to viewing babies with disabilities or babies of color as less desirable.

Many couples undergo genetic testing to see if a fetus carries any hereditary predisposition to specific diseases or birth. To have a second child, some couples traveled to Hong Kong, a region of China where the policy was not enforced.

By the late 1980s, the Chinese government had changed its mind about the policy. Leaders feared that a dearth of girl babies would eventually result in fewer grown women for men to marry. Leaders also worried that too many elderly would be left without offspring to care for them. They feared as well that the one-child policy would result in too few young people for the workforce. To deal with these concerns, the government relaxed the law in 1989, permitting parents to have a second child if both parents were themselves only children. But by 2012, China still had about forty million more men than women. The law was again changed in 2013, to allow couples to have a second child when either parent was an only child. So far a baby boom has not occurred. In interviews, Chinese parents express reluctance about having a second child due to the high cost of living.

genetic disorders, such as Down syndrome. Many couples choose an abortion if the fetus's medical condition is severe. Antiabortion groups oppose genetic testing because it often leads to abortion. Even some people who support abortion are unsure about the ethics of sex selection and genetic testing, since the procedures raise concerns about unjustly weeding out potential lives that are not perfect. As of June 2015, seven states prohibit sex selection abortions. One state, North Dakota, prohibits abortions for genetic disorders, even those where the fetus may die before or shortly after birth.

REPRODUCTIVE TOURISM

The for-profit aspect of the ART industry creates other ethical concerns. In the United States, fertility clinics advertise on radio and television, in newspapers, and on the Internet. Many make claims of success that can't be proven. The high cost of ART in some countries and a confusing web of laws and regulations around the globe have led to a global phenomenon called reproductive tourism. For example, in countries such as Australia and Canada, buying human eggs for IVF implantation is illegal. In other countries, such as Italy, the use of IVF is restricted to heterosexual couples. Citizens in these nations who can afford the cost of travel and ART will frequently have the procedure in the United States, where the practice is legal and available to a broad range of individuals.

American citizens also take advantage of reproductive tourism. For example, US couples looking for a woman to carry and give birth to a baby for them—a practice known as surrogacy—frequently hire surrogates in India. Usually a couple's fertilized egg is implanted into a surrogate woman. In other cases, sperm alone (not a fertilized egg) is used to induce a surrogate's pregnancy, in which case the surrogate is also the genetic mother of the baby. In the United States, surrogacy is mostly unregulated, and the cost of hiring a woman to be a surrogate varies from about $75,000 to $120,000 per pregnancy. But in India, surrogacy fees are much lower, ranging from $25,000 to $30,000 per pregnancy. Many people question the economic ethics of carrying someone else's baby. Generally, the people who hire a surrogate have money, while most surrogates are poor. Surrogates are easily exploited, especially if they are signing a contract in a language they don't understand. During the nine months of pregnancy, many surrogates in India are required to follow regulations that restrict their freedom. They have to live in apartments away from their families, follow a specified diet, and avoid travel and contact with friends and family. They sign away all rights to an abortion and to seeking medical attention outside of the fertility clinic that has arranged the surrogacy deal. Cesarean sections (delivering a baby by cutting through the abdomen and uterus) are frequently not medically necessary. Yet many surrogates undergo the procedure because the contracting parents find it easier to plan for the baby's arrival, since the operation is scheduled for a specific time and day, as opposed to a natural birth, which might not take place on the expected due date. Cesarean sections pose a greater risk to the surrogates and their babies than natural deliveries. And for the surrogates, natural childbirth in later pregnancies may not be possible after an initial surgical delivery.

Several countries, such as France, the United Kingdom, Australia, and Canada, have banned commercial surrogacy. Reproductive rights groups advocate for developing global regulations of ART practices in an ethical and fair manner.

The nations that top the list for providing surrogate motherhood services include the United States, India, Thailand, Ukraine, and Russia. This first-time surrogate mother lives in a temporary home for surrogate mothers provided by an IVF center about 44 miles (70 kilometers) from the Indian city of Ahmedabad.

CHILDHOOD PREGNANCIES

In 1994 the United Nations hosted the International Conference on Population and Development (ICPD) in Cairo, Egypt. At the conference, global delegates drew up a document stating that governments should provide reproductive rights, including the right of couples and individuals to decide the number of children they want and when they will have them, the right to information about reproductive decisions, and the right of access to high-quality sexual and reproductive health care. In addition, the conference document recognized people's right to make these decisions "free of discrimination, coercion [force] and violence, as expressed in human rights documents." Numerous international treaties, conventions, and policies have since expanded these rights.

Despite these international agreements, pregnancy rates are high among girls and women whose cultural or ethnic backgrounds restrict their freedoms and among those with limited access to reproductive health services and information. Twenty thousand of these young women give birth every day. About 19 percent of young women in developing countries are pregnant before they reach the age of eighteen, and of this group, more than 30 percent are under the age of fifteen. For these girls, complications of pregnancy and childbirth are the leading causes of death.

Many girls around the world become pregnant as a result of sexual abuse or rape. In general, girls growing up in rural areas and in poverty and those who are denied education are more likely to become pregnant than educated, urban girls growing up in more affluent families.

Other factors, such as a culture's views of women's roles in society, influence whether a woman becomes pregnant. Research shows that the more education a girl receives, the

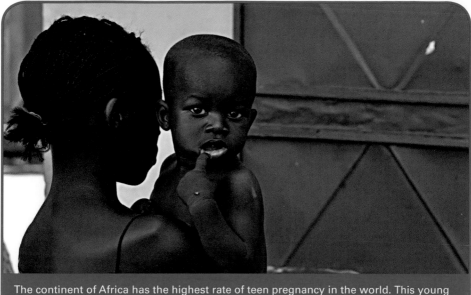

The continent of Africa has the highest rate of teen pregnancy in the world. This young woman and her baby live in Mali, where a majority of the population is under twenty-five years old and more than 40 percent of all girls between the ages of fifteen and nineteen are pregnant or are already mothers.

more likely she is to put off pregnancy and to have fewer children overall. Educated women most often use contraception, choose to have smaller families, receive better health care, and earn money to support their children. In turn, greater education allows women to be better parents. In fact, research shows that an educated woman may be the best prescription for ending the cycle of poverty that is often passed down from mother to child. For example, in many parts of the world, such as rural China, parents do not even consider sending their girls to school. They assume the girls will end up working in the fields and do not need an education. They would rather spend money on educating their sons, who would then be qualified for higher-paying jobs. And in Cambodia, parents who don't have much money would rather spend their limited funds on their sons' education.

Girl Brides

Clarisse is a fourteen-year-old girl in Chad, a nation in central Africa. Like many adolescents in developing countries, she lives where marriages are forced on young girls and childhood births are expected. She has no control over when she will become pregnant. "I was 14," she explained. "My mom and her sisters began to prepare food, and my dad asked my brothers, sisters and me to wear our best clothes because we were about to have a party. Because I didn't know what was going on, I celebrated

Like Clarisse, this young girl from India is a child bride. South Asia has the largest number of child brides, and globally one in nine girls will be married before the age of fifteen.

like everyone else. It was that day I learned that it was my wedding and that I had to join my husband. I tried to escape but was caught. So I found myself with a husband three times older than me. . . . Ten months later, I found myself with a baby in my arms."

MATERNAL MORTALITY

Thousands of pregnant women and girls around the world die each year, particularly in developing countries in Africa, Asia, Latin America, and eastern Europe. The World Health Organization (WHO) is dedicated to promoting the highest standards of health worldwide. WHO reported that from 1990 to 2010, "every two minutes, a woman [died] of pregnancy-related complications." In total, according to WHO data, 289,000 expectant women died from medical complications due to pregnancy and childbirth in 2013. Medical problems in developing countries are due to poverty, a lack of rural health clinics, and few trained doctors and nurses. But beyond physical reasons for maternal deaths lie cultural issues that are difficult to overcome. The primary cultural issue is that women in these countries are considered second-class citizens. Without equal access to schooling and literacy, they are not empowered to demand basic medical care. Dr. Mahmoud F. Fathalla, a noted Egyptian obstetrician and advocate for reproductive human rights for women, wrote, "Women are not dying because of untreatable diseases. They are dying because societies have yet to make the decision that their lives are worth saving."

Sub-Saharan Africa has the greatest number of maternal deaths: 179,000 women per year, or 62 percent of worldwide maternal deaths. A woman living in this region of the world has a one in thirty-eight chance of dying in childbirth during her lifetime. The most common complications leading to death are bleeding and infections after childbirth, pregnancy-related high blood pressure, and unsafe abortions. According to WHO, 30 women out of every 100,000 die yearly from unsafe abortions in developed countries. But the numbers jump dramatically in the developing world, where

220 women out of 100,000 die yearly from unsafe abortions. In sub-Saharan Africa alone, about half of the women who undergo unsafe abortions die.

But some poor countries have made great strides. For example, Sri Lanka, a country with one of the lowest per capita incomes worldwide, has lowered its maternal mortality rate from 550 maternal deaths for every 100,000 live births to 58 over the last fifty years. As journalists Nicholas Kristof and Sheryl WuDunn have written, "Sri Lanka invests in health and education generally, and pays particular attention to gender equality. Some 89 percent of Sri Lankan women are literate, compared to just 43 percent across South Asia."

In general, the United States and other developed regions in the world have a lower ratio of maternal deaths (16 women die for every 100,000 live births) than developing countries (230 deaths per 100,000 live births). In the developing nation of India, for example, the maternal death ratio is high (190 deaths for every 100,000 live births). WHO states that "ninety-nine per cent of maternal deaths occur in developing countries; most could have been prevented with proven interventions," such as prenatal, birth, postdelivery, and emergency care by trained medical professionals.

Within the developed world, western European countries have lower childbirth death rates than the United States, where there are twenty-eight deaths per one hundred thousand live births. For example, in Italy and Sweden, there are four deaths per one hundred thousand live births. According to UN statistics released in 2010, the United States places fiftieth in the world for maternal mortality. This low ranking is mostly due to lack of access to effective health care by American women of color and low-income women.

Global funding for reproductive services is critical to lowering maternal mortality rates. The amount of US foreign aid to developing countries has been greatly limited by abortion politics. In 1984 US president Ronald Reagan issued what became known as the global gag rule. The rule was formulated at a population conference in Mexico City. It denied US aid to foreign reproductive health clinics where abortion was advised or discussed, even for women whose health was at risk. In the following decades, the rule was kicked back and forth, depending on the politics of the US president in office. In January 2009, President Barack Obama revoked the gag rule. He also announced funding support for the United Nations Population Fund (UNFPA), a UN organization that provides family planning and reproductive services around the world.

MAKING PROGRESS

Even with high rates of maternal mortality worldwide, the overall global rate has declined 45 percent since 1990. To continue to address the issue and to improve other serious global health issues related to factors such as poverty, hunger, and disease, the United Nations initiated the Global Strategy for Women's and Children's Health (GSWCH) in 2000. GSWCH Goal 5 aims to prevent thirty-three million unwanted pregnancies and to save the lives of women dying during pregnancy, childbirth, and unsafe abortions by 2015. Strategies for successful reduction of these rates include increasing access to good-quality reproductive health care and family planning, contraception, prenatal care, and the prevalence of health professionals to assist in labor and delivery.

Individuals as well as governments are responding to the

Edna Adan Ismail founded the Edna Adan Maternity Hospital in Hargeisa, Somaliland, to serve pregnant women. She is also a vocal opponent of female circumcision (sometimes referred to as genital mutilation), which involves the removal of some or all of a woman's external genitalia. The procedure—common in Africa, some regions of the Middle East, and parts of Asia—can lead to serious complications during childbirth and to deadly bleeding.

needs of maternal health in developing countries. For example, Edna Adan, a trained nurse and midwife, sold her car and many other possessions to fulfill her dream of building and opening a hospital for women in Hargeisa, Somaliland, in 2002. In Somaliland, in eastern Africa where Adan grew up, most women go through pregnancy without a health professional monitoring the baby's development and the woman's overall health. Only 10 percent of mothers in Somaliland deliver their babies with help from a trained midwife. In the event of a complication—if a woman hemorrhages or needs a cesarean section, for example—the woman and her baby often die. Somaliland has one of the highest maternal and infant mortality rates worldwide, with one thousand to fourteen hundred maternal deaths per one hundred thousand live births and with seventy-three infant deaths for each one thousand births.

Building the hospital was just the first step for Adan. Next, she began training nurses and midwives. Many work in the surrounding communities, where each midwife may deliver up to four hundred babies a year. After thirteen years of hard work, Adan and her staff have increased the survival rate of pregnant women and babies in Somaliland by 75 percent.

SEX EDUCATION

According to extensive studies by the Guttmacher Institute, most women choose abortion because of an unintended pregnancy. In 2008 unsafe abortions killed forty-seven thousand women worldwide. The WHO points to three key ways that unsafe abortion can be prevented and controlled: "good sexuality education; prevention of unintended pregnancy through use of effective contraception, including emergency contraception; and provision of safe, legal abortion."

In the twenty-first century, the United States has one of the highest rates of adolescent pregnancy among all developed nations. According to the WHO, one of the lowest rates of teen pregnancy occurs in the Netherlands, where sex education starts in lower grades and family planning services are widely accessible. Sex education in countries with low teen pregnancy rates is aimed at concrete ways of preventing pregnancy. Much of the focus is also on empowering adolescents to make good decisions about their sexual well-being.

In the United States, the CDC reports that girls who drop out of high school are more likely to get pregnant than those who stay in school. The children of teen mothers are also at greater risk for teenage pregnancy, dropping out of school, behavior and medical problems, and unemployment. All the same, US government leaders, parents, teachers, and school principals are divided over teaching sex education in public schools. If sex education is offered at all, it typically falls into

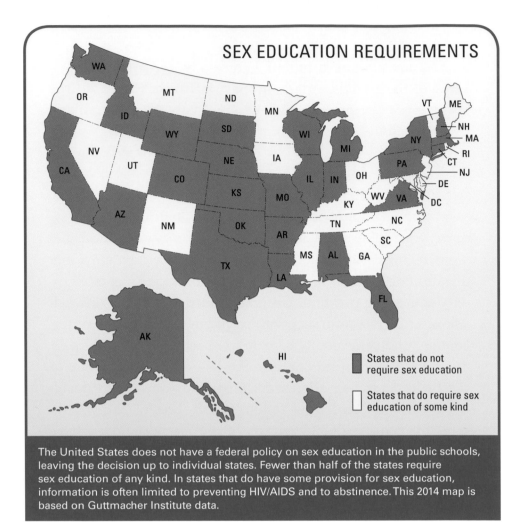

■ States that do not require sex education

☐ States that do require sex education of some kind

The United States does not have a federal policy on sex education in the public schools, leaving the decision up to individual states. Fewer than half of the states require sex education of any kind. In states that do have some provision for sex education, information is often limited to preventing HIV/AIDS and to abstinence. This 2014 map is based on Guttmacher Institute data.

one extreme or the other: abstinence-only-until-marriage or comprehensive sex education.

Those Americans who support abstinence-only-until-marriage programs say that abstinence is the only effective way of preventing pregnancy and avoiding STDs. To be eligible for federal funds to pay for abstinence-only programs, state sex education programs must follow specific guidelines. These include teaching the positive health and emotional benefits of abstinence. They also include teaching that sex outside of marriage produces negative emotional and physical consequences.

Advocates of comprehensive sexuality education support teaching about birth control methods and emergency contraception along with abstinence. According to the Sexuality Information and Education Council of the United States (SIECUS), comprehensive sexuality education also includes teaching about individual choices regarding reproduction, relationships, LGBT topics, and anatomy and puberty. Comprehensive programs are dedicated to providing information that is scientifically and medically accurate.

Various studies have been unable to verify that the rate of sexual abstinence is actually increased through abstinence-only sex education programs. In fact, research shows that postponing sexual intercourse is a more likely outcome of comprehensive sex education programs. So is increasing the numbers of students using condoms and other birth control methods and decreasing the number of partners with whom a student engages in sex. All of these behaviors not only reduce the risk of pregnancy, but they also reduce transmission of STDs.

The US government does not mandate sex education in public schools. As a result, only twenty-two states and the District of Columbia require programs in sex education. Where sex education is offered, twenty-five states require that abstinence be stressed, and nineteen states require that students be taught about the importance of delaying sex until marriage.

In 2009 President Barack Obama launched two federal programs advancing comprehensive sexuality education: the President's Teen Pregnancy Prevention Initiative and the Personal Responsibility Education Program. States that receive funding for these voluntary programs must provide information that is medically accurate. They must also teach about specific topics, including HIV/AIDS, STDs, and contraception.

GETTING THE WORD OUT

Many states are successfully addressing sex education in a variety of ways. For example, the state of Washington's Healthy Youth Act and the Proven Programs Act require that sex education programs teach about abstinence as well as contraception. These programs are based on medically and scientifically accurate and effective information that is appropriate for all ages, genders, and sexual orientations. California, North Carolina, and Oregon have similar laws. Although Colorado does not require comprehensive sex education, the state does not permit schools to use federal funds for abstinence-only programs. State-run teen pregnancy prevention programs in Massachusetts and Pennsylvania have focused attention on adolescents with the highest rates of pregnancy, such as African American and Latina teens in low-income areas of the states.

Youth activists are fired up about their rights to accurate and effective sex information. For example, Advocates for Youth is a global organization that works to promote adolescent sexual health. It trains youth through its Youth Activist Network (YAN) to reach out to other young people around the world. Through an online website called Amplify, these activists motivate others to provide sexual health information to their peers. More than seventy-five thousand youths have joined YAN worldwide.

CONCLUSION

Anthony Comstock, Margaret Sanger, Mary Ware Dennett, Dr. Gregory Pincus, Gloria Steinem, Sarah Weddington, and

Dr. Willie Parker are just a few of the people who tell the story of reproductive rights in the United States. From ancient times, when people turned to magic potions to prevent pregnancy, to the revolution of the Pill in the 1960s, the establishment of a constitutional right to abortion in the 1970s, and the radically new reproductive technologies of the twenty-first century, men and women have looked to better understand and control their reproductive health and the size of their families. Debate over availability of, access to, and funding for contraception, sex education, and abortion has roiled the United States for centuries, leading to controversial legal and political rulings, heated and passionate arguments, and even lethal violence. As society changes and as technologies continue to evolve and expand the possibilities for childbearing and individual control over reproduction, Americans and other global citizens will continue to debate and discuss what it means to be a parent.

GLOSSARY

abortion: the deliberate termination of a pregnancy. Techniques for ending a pregnancy depend on the stage of pregnancy and on various local and federal laws and regulations. Procedures typically include either surgical extraction of a fetus in a clinic or hospital setting or a medical abortion involving pharmaceutical drugs that bring on the end of the pregnancy.

abstinence: refraining from sexual activity, mostly as a way to avoid pregnancy

assisted reproductive technologies (ART): a wide range of advanced techniques that offer infertile individuals or couples the possibility of conceiving a child. The most common form of ART is in vitro fertilization, which involves fertilizing a woman's egg with a man's sperm outside the body and implanting the fertilized egg in the woman's uterus. Fertility drugs are often part of the process to trigger or better regulate ovulation, the release of an egg from a woman's ovary. ART is a costly process, typically not covered by US insurance companies, and is therefore an option for very few couples.

contraception: the wide range of devices and techniques that people have used over the centuries to prevent pregnancy. Behavioral approaches range from abstinence (no sex at all) to the rhythm method (having sex only at the point in a woman's menstrual cycle in which she is least fertile) and withdrawal, in which a man removes the penis from the vagina before orgasm and ejaculation. Devices include various items such as condoms to cover the penis during sex, diaphragms (silicone cups that cover the cervix), and intrauterine devices (IUDs), which a doctor implants in a woman's uterus. Hormone-based techniques include the Pill (taken on a daily basis) and contraceptive injections and implants, which prevent pregnancy for a matter of weeks or years rather than hours. Contraception is also known as birth control.

in vitro fertilization (IVF): an advanced reproductive technique in which fertilization of a woman's egg with a man's sperm occurs outside the body rather than through sexual intercourse. Doctors at fertility clinics perform the procedure to collect a woman's eggs and a man's sperm and mix them together. When embryos have grown, the woman returns to the clinic, where a doctor will implant them into her uterus. Fertility drugs are often part of the process to trigger or better regulate ovulation. IVF does not guarantee a pregnancy.

pessary: a removable cap placed over a woman's cervix to block semen from entering the uterus. In the ancient world, they were made from plant fibers, roots, and crushed herbs, soaked in honey, oil, and fruit juices that acted as spermicides. Nineteenth-century pessaries were known by many names, including womb veils. In the twenty-first century, the caps, usually diaphragms, are typically made of latex or silicone and are used in conjunction with spermicide jellies or foams.

preimplantation genetic diagnosis (PGD): an assisted reproductive technology that allows doctors to identify genetic defects within embryos that have been created through in vitro fertilization before implanting them into a woman's uterus. In cases where PGD reveals genetic disorders, a woman can decide against implantation, thereby preventing the passing of certain diseases and disorders to the child.

prophylactic: a medicine, device, or procedure that prevents disease or pregnancy. In birth control scenarios, common prophylactics include condoms. While preventing sperm from entering the uterus, they also protect both sexual partners from sexually transmitted infections.

reproductive justice: a global social justice movement that focuses on issues of importance to all advocates of reproductive rights, including communities of color. These issues include economic justice, the environment, immigrants' rights, disability rights, and discrimination based on race and sexual orientation. While reproductive justice works to ensure that reproductive legal rights are accessible to all women, it also focuses more broadly on a woman's right to raise a family in a healthy environment, to have access to affordable day care, to be free of sexual exploitation, to earn a living wage, and to protect other basic human rights that impact all women and their families.

sterilization: a surgical form of permanent birth control. During a tubal ligation—a sterilization surgery performed on a woman—a doctor surgically closes or blocks the fallopian tubes so that the eggs can never come in contact with a man's semen. A man can be sterilized too, by surgically cutting or blocking the tubes that carry sperm from the testicles to the penis. This procedure is known as a vasectomy.

surrogacy: going through a pregnancy and delivering a child for someone else. A traditional surrogate is a woman who agrees to be artificially inseminated with a man's sperm. If she becomes pregnant, she carries and gives birth to the baby, who will then be raised by the man and his partner. The woman who gives birth to the baby is its biological mother, although most surrogates give up legal rights to that child. A gestational surrogate is a woman who has no biological ties to the child. She agrees to be implanted with the embryo created through in vitro fertilization of another man and woman. If she becomes pregnant and delivers the child, the gestational surrogate is the birth mother, and the biological mother is the woman whose egg was fertilized.

ultrasound: ultrasound imaging, also called ultrasound scanning or sonography, involves a small probe and gel placed directly on the skin in a clinic setting. High-frequency sound waves are transmitted from the probe through the gel into the body. A computer uses the sound waves that bounce back to create an image (sonogram) of a patient's internal organs, blood vessels, or fetus in real time. Ultrasounds enable physicians to monitor the health of a patient or of a fetus.

viability: the minimum age at which a fetus can survive outside the womb. In the United States, this is medically and legally defined as the twenty-fourth week of pregnancy.

ca. 20,000–5,500 years ago: The most common means of preventing pregnancy is abortion. Myths, superstitions, and recipes for creating magic and herbal potions are passed down orally.

ca. 1784–1300 BCE: The Egyptians record methods for contraception and abortion in the Egyptian Ramesseum Papyrus IV, the Ebers Papyrus, and the Berlin Papyrus. Substances used for contraception include crocodile dung and fermented dough.

ca. 350 BCE: The Greek philosopher Aristotle advocates abortion for population control and advocates spermicides containing cedar and olive oils for contraception.

ca. 23–138 CE: The Greeks and Romans write about contraception and abortion methods, including potions, liniments, and pessaries. Substances used for contraception and abortion include pennyroyal and other herbs, figs and other fruits, and sticky substances such as honey.

ca. 865–1037: Persian physicians such as al-Razi and Ibn Sina (Avicenna) advise the use of crushed herbs, fruit juices, and oils for contraception. Contraceptive devices include suppositories, tampons, and oral potions.

ca. 500–1500: The Roman Catholic Church advocates celibacy for priests and abstinence for its followers.

1600–1700s: Puritan and Protestant settlers leave reproduction to "God's will." By the end of the eighteenth century, the most common birth control methods are coitus interruptus, prolonged breast-feeding, and abortion.

Early 1800s: Abortions before quickening are legal in the United States under Common Law.

1821: Connecticut becomes the first state to criminalize abortions that occur after quickening.

1830s–1870s: Ann Trow Lohman (a.k.a. Madame Restell) and more than two hundred other abortionists operate in New York City. Abortion rates climb, and the practice becomes commonplace.

1831: Social reformer Robert Dale Owen advocates population control and male sexual restraint in *Moral Physiology*. Years later, he advises coitus interruptus as the most reliable birth control technique.

1832: Charles Knowlton, a Boston physician, prescribes the withdrawal method in his book *Fruits of Philosophy*. In later editions, he advocates douching.

1839: Charles Goodyear develops a process for vulcanizing rubber, setting the stage for a host of rubber contraceptive devices, such as condoms, womb veils, and douching apparatuses.

1847: Doctors organize the American Medical Association, which later crusades against abortion.

1850–1870s: Advice literature, public lectures, and advertisements for contraception create an aura of public acceptance for contraception and abortion. Many Americans, however, are uncomfortable with the public display of sexuality and with the idea that sex can be separated from reproduction.

1870s: Feminist groups advocate for voluntary motherhood and promote sexual abstinence.

1873: Anthony Comstock successfully lobbies the US Congress to pass the Comstock Act, which criminalizes the mailing of "obscene, lewd, or lascivious" material, including information about and items used for contraception and abortion. Many states criminalize possession and sale of these items. In 1879 Connecticut criminalizes the use of contraception. Comstock helps form the New York Society for the Suppression of Vice and as an agent of the US Postal Service arrests purveyors of contraceptive devices.

1880: Abortion has become criminalized in most states, regardless of the stage of pregnancy. Many women use illegal and drastic measures to carry out abortions.

1914: Margaret Sanger, a nurse, begins to challenge the Comstock laws after Anthony Comstock shuts down her column about STDs in the *New York Call*. Sanger fights for the right of doctors to dispense contraception to women for medical purposes.

1915: Mary Ware Dennett and other women form the National Birth Control League and fight for the removal of contraception from state and federal obscenity laws.

1916: Sanger and her sister Ethel Byrne open a birth control clinic in the Brownsville section of Brooklyn (New York) in defiance of the law.

1918: The New York Court of Appeals interprets New York penal law as permitting women to obtain contraceptives for health reasons, with a physician's prescription, but few New York physicians prescribe contraception. Mary Ware Dennett publishes *The Sex Side of Life*, a sex education pamphlet.

1920: The Nineteenth Amendment to the US Constitution, which gives American women the right to vote, is ratified.

1927: The US Supreme Court upholds Virginia's sterilization law in the case of *Buck v. Bell*. By mid-century, thirty-two states require sterilization for people with insanity, mental retardation, and other conditions thought to be inherited.

1929: Mary Ware Dennett is arrested for writing *The Sex Side of Life*. In 1930 the US Court of Appeals for the Second Circuit holds that sex information is not obscene.

1930: Pope Pius XI issues the *Casti Connubii* prohibiting all artificial forms of birth control for Catholic women and promoting the use of the rhythm method.

1936: In *United States v. One Package*, the US Court of Appeals for the Second Circuit holds that contraceptive articles are not obscene, essentially gutting the Comstock Act. However, women still need a doctor's prescription to obtain contraception.

1939: The Birth Control Federation of America is formed. It later becomes the Planned Parenthood Federation of America.

1942: In *Skinner v. State of Oklahoma*, the US Supreme Court states that marriage and procreation are fundamental rights.

1951–1957: Margaret Sanger convinces Dr. Gregory Pincus to conduct research for the development of a birth control pill. Pincus works with Dr. John Rock, who tests the pill in clinical trials. Katharine McCormick funds the pill's development.

1957: The FDA approves Enovid, a pill for menstrual problems. The pill is prescribed to thousands of women for off-label birth control purposes.

1960: The FDA approves Enovid for contraception. Within five years, more than six million American women are taking the Pill.

1963: Pope Paul VI issues the *Humanae Vitae*, prohibiting the use of birth control pills by Catholic women.

1965: In *Griswold v. Connecticut*, the US Supreme Court strikes down a Connecticut law criminalizing the use of contraceptives, ruling that the law violates a married couple's right to privacy.

1972: In *Eisenstadt v. Baird*, the US Supreme Court extends the right to privacy established by *Griswold* to unmarried couples.

1973: In *Roe v. Wade*, the US Supreme Court holds that the right to privacy encompasses a woman's decision to end a pregnancy. A woman's right to an abortion before viability is absolute.

1977: The US Congress enacts the Hyde Amendment, which restricts federal funding for abortion.

1992: In *Planned Parenthood v. Casey*, the US Supreme Court rules that a state can limit a woman's right to an abortion before viability, as long as the restriction does not create an "undue burden" on women.

1993–2009. Antiabortion extremists murder eight abortion providers and clinic workers.

1994:
In an attempt to curb violence at abortion clinics, the US Congress passes the Freedom of Access to Clinic Entrances Act.

The International Conference on Population and Development in Egypt states that governments worldwide must secure human rights by providing reproductive rights.

2000–2015: Assisted reproductive technologies (ART), first developed in 1978 with in vitro fertilization, is used to determine the sex of a fetus, leading to the abortions of certain babies—mostly female. Reproductive tourism and surrogacy create other ethical and moral concerns.

2003: The federal Partial Birth Abortion Act, which bans D&X abortion procedures, is signed into law.

2010: The US Congress passes the Affordable Care Act, which authorizes insurance coverage for contraception.

2010–2015: As of July 1, 2015, states have passed 282 TRAP laws restricting women's access to abortion, forcing many clinic closures.

2014:
In *Burwell v. Hobby Lobby Stores, Inc.*, the US Supreme Court holds that owners of a family-owned business with strong Christian beliefs did not have to pay for health insurance coverage for contraception they likened to abortion.

Despite the high incidence of maternal mortality worldwide, the overall global rate declines. The United States continues to have one of the highest adolescent rates of pregnancy in the developed world. Although sex education remains controversial among Americans, many states and nonprofit organizations develop comprehensive sex education programs for adolescents.

2015:
In *Whole Woman's Health v. Cole*, the US Court of Appeals for the Fifth Circuit upheld a Texas law requiring that abortion providers have admitting privileges at local hospitals and that clinics meet the same hospital-like building standards as surgical centers handling riskier procedures. In June 2015, the US Supreme Court blocked enforcement of this ruling pending possible Supreme Court review.

In *Jackson Women's Health Organization v. Currier*, the US Court of Appeals for the Fifth Circuit blocked a Mississippi law that required abortion providers to have admitting privileges at hospitals and that would have closed the last remaining abortion clinic in the state. Mississippi has asked the US Supreme Court to review the case.

SOURCE NOTES

9 "*Roe* at 40: New Infographics Illustrate Key Facts about Abortion in the United States," Guttmacher Institute, January 8, 2013, http://www.guttmacher.org/media/inthenews/2013/01/08/.

9 Norman E. Himes, *Medical History of Contraception* (1936; repr., New York: Schocken, 1970), xiv.

10 *Grundriss der Medizin der alten Ägypter* 1958, 4, pt. 1, p. 277; 4, pt. 2, p. 211; 5:476–478 (hierglyphs text), in John M. Riddle, *Contraception and Abortion from the Ancient World to the Renaissance* (Cambridge, MA: Harvard University Press, 1992), 66.

10 Karen Jensen, *Reproduction: The Cycle of Life* (Washington, DC: U.S. News Books, 1957), 26.

13 *Grundriss*, 6:277; 5:476 (hieroglyphs text); 4, pt. 2, p. 211, and Five Ramesseum Papyri 1956, p. 25, N. to C. 3; and Grundriss, 4, pt. 1, p. 277; pt. 2, p. 210; 5:476, in Riddle, *Contraception and Abortion*, 69.

13 Ibid., 4, pt. 1, pp. 279–280; pt. 2, p. 212; 5:480–481 (hierglyphs text), in Riddle, *Contraception and Abortion*, 72.

14 Riddle, *Contraception and Abortion*, 18.

14 Aristotle, *Politics*, 7.16.15.1335b19-26, in Riddle, *Contraception and Abortion*, 18.

14 D'Arcy Wentworth Thompson, ed., *Works of Aristotle*, vol. IV, *Historia Animalium* (Oxford, 1910), iv, 583a, in Himes, *Medical History*, 80.

14 Hippocrates, *De mulierum affectibus*, 1.76, in Riddle, *Contraception and Abortion*, 74.

15 Ibn Sina, *Canon of Avicenna*, chapter on the Prevention of Conception, in Himes, *Medical History*, 142.

15 *Juris anglicani*, 1.23.10, 12, in Riddle, *Contraception and Abortion*, 140.

17 John D'Emilio and Estelle B. Freedman, *Intimate Matters: A History of Sexuality in America*, 3rd ed. (Chicago: University of Chicago Press, 2012), 25.

18 Janet Farrell Brodie, *Contraception and Abortion in 19th-Century America* (Ithaca, NY: Cornell University Press, 1994), 42.

19 Sarah Jay to Kitty Livingston, July 16, 1783, John Jay Papers, Rare Book and Manuscript Library, Columbia University, New York City, in Mary Beth Norton, *Liberty's Daughters: The Revolutionary Experience of American Women, 1750–1800* (Ithaca, NY: Cornell University Press, 1980), 77.

20 Dorothy Roberts, *Killing the Black Body: Race, Reproduction, and the Meaning of Liberty* (New York: Vintage, 1999), 10.

22 John Todd, quoted in Shirley Green, *The Curious History of Contraception* (London: Ebury Press, 1971), 14, in Andrea Tone, *Devices and Desires: A History of Contraceptives in America* (New York: Farrar, Straus and Giroux, 2002), 15.

24 Charles Knowlton, *Fruits of Philosophy* (1839), 8, in Brodie, *Contraception and Abortion in 19th-Century America*, 97.

24 Charles Knowlton, *A History of the Recent Excitement in Ashfield* (Ashfield, MA), n.p., 1834, in Brodie, *Contraception and Abortion in 19th-Century America*, 4.

24–25 Ibid., 95.

25 Thomas Low Nichols, *Esoteric Anthropology* (1853), 151, in Brodie, *Contraception and Abortion in 19th-Century America*, 127.

26 George Napheys, *The Physical Life of Woman* (1872), 91–99, in Brodie,

Contraception and Abortion in 19th-Century America, 183.

26 Ibid.

27 Frederick Hollick, *The Origin of Life* (1846), Preface, in Brodie, *Contraception and Abortion in 19th-Century America*, 116.

28 W. E. B. Du Bois, B*lack Reconstruction in America, 1860–1880*, ed. August Meier (New York: Atheneum, 1985), 44, in Roberts, *Killing the Black Body*, 24.

28 Roberts, *Killing the Black Body*, 27.

29 Herbert G. Gutman, *Black Family in Slavery and Freedom, 1750–1925* (New York: Pantheon, 1976), 80, in Roberts, *Killing the Black Body*, 47.

29 Ibid.

29 Charles L. Perdue, Thomas E. Barden, and Robert K. Phillips, eds., *Weevils in the Wheat: Interviews with Virginia Ex-Slaves* (Charlottesville: University Press of Virginia, 1976), 48–49, in Roberts, *Killing the Black Body*, 45.

31 Lewis Perry, *Childhood, Marriage, and Reform: Henry Clarke Wright, 1797-1870* (Chicago: University of Chicage Press, 1980), 70, 232, 231, and Henry Clarke Wright, *The Unwelcome Child* (1985), letter 5, in Brodie, *Contraception and Abortion in the 19th-Century America*, 112.

31 Ibid.

32 Ibid.

32 *Woman's Advocate* (Dayton, Ohio) 1, no. 20 (April 8, 1869): 16, in James C. Mohr, *Abortion in America: The Origins and Evolution of National Policy* (New York: Oxford University Press, 1978), 112.

34 *Boston Daily Times*, January 4–11, 1845, in Mohr, *Abortion in America*, 48.

36–37 Horatio R. Storer, *Why Not? A Book for Every Woman, the Prize Essay . . .* (Boston: Lea and Shepard, 1866), 85, in Carroll Smith-Rosenberg, *Disorderly Conduct: Visions of Gender in Victorian America* (New York: Oxford University Press, 1985), 238.

38 Ezra Heywood, *Uncivil Liberty: An Essay to Show the Injustice and Impolicy of Ruling Woman without Her Consent* (Princeton, MA: Cooperative, 1872), 21, in Tone, *Devices and Desires*, 15.

39 Tone, *Devices and Desires*, 5.

40 George P. Sanger, ed., *The Statutes at Large and Proclamations of the United States of America XVII*, chapter CCLVIII, an Act for the Suppression of Trade, in, and Circulation of, Obscene Literature and Articles of Immoral Use, section 2, section 148 (Boston: Little, Brown, 1873), 599.

40 Ibid.

40 Ibid., section 1, 598.

42 Elizabeth Hampsten, ed., *Read This Only to Yourself: The Private Writings of Midwestern Women, 1880–1910* (Bloomington: Indiana University Press, 1982), 104, in Tone, *Devices and Desires*, 44.

42 Tone, *Devices and Desires*, 31.

43 New York Society for the Suppression of Vice (NYSSV), Obscene Matter Confiscated, bin 3, 403, Library of Congress, Manuscript Division.

44 Margaret Sanger, *The Autobiography of Margaret Sanger*, originally published as *Margaret Sanger: An Autobiography* (1938; repr., New York: Dover, 1971), 89.

44 Ibid., 88.

45 Ibid., 90.

45 Ibid., 91.

46 Ibid., 76.

47 Ibid., 77.

47 Ibid., 117.

47 Ibid., 120.

48 Constance M. Chen, "The Sex Side of Life": *Mary Ware Dennett's Pioneering Battle for Birth Control and Sex Education* (New York: New Press, 1996), 194.

49 Ibid., 212.

49 Ibid., 176.

50 David M. Kennedy, *Birth Control in America: The Career of Margaret Sanger* (New Haven, CT: Yale University Press, 1973), 220.

50 *The Consolidated Laws of New York, Annotated*, New York Penal Law, L. 1909, chapter 88, Indecency, section 1142, Indecent Articles, 1916 (Northport, NY: Edward Thompson, 1917), 417–418.

50 Ibid., chapter 88, Indecency, section 1145, Physicians' Instruments, 1916, 419.

50 Sanger, *The Autobiography of Margaret Sanger*, 212.

52 "Mrs. Byrne Sinking Fast, Sister Warns," *New York Tribune*, January 29, 1917, 1, http://search.proquest .com/hnpnewyorktribunefull/docview /575663934/fulltextPDF/869968A5C93 84D16PQ/1?accountid = 147304.

52 "Mrs. Byrne Now Fed by Force," *New York Times*, January 28, 1917, 1, http://timesmachine.nytimes.com /timesmachine/1917/01/2/102314787 .html?pageNumber = 1.

52 Ibid., 6.

52 Tone, *Devices and Desires*, 108.

53 Margaret Sanger, *The New Motherhood* (London: J. Cape, 1922), 120, in Tone, *Devices and Desires*, 108.

54 Josephus Daniels to W. L. Stoddard, February 12, 1915, box 2140, General Correspondence, Records of the Bureau of Medicine and Surgery, RG 52, National Archives, in Tone, *Devices and Desires*, 91.

54 Tone, *Devices and Desires*, 91.

54 "Keeping Fit to Fight" (Washington, 1918), 1; "Syllabus Accredited for Use in Official Supplementary Lectures on Sex Hygiene and Venereal Diseases," unpublished typescript (February 1918), National Archives, Record Group 165, Box 433, in Allan M. Brandt, *No Magic Bullet: A Social History of Venereal Disease in the United States since 1880* (New York: Oxford University Press, 1985), 62.

55 Leisa D. Meyer, "Creating G.I. Jane: The Regulation of Sexuality and Sexual Behavior in the Women's Army Corps during World War II," *Feminist Studies* 18, no. 3 (Autumn 1992): 581.

56 Tone, *Devices and Desires*, 144.

56 Ibid.

56 *Buck v. Bell*, 274 U.S. 200, 207 (1927).

56 *Skinner v. State of Oklahoma*, 316 U.S. 535, 541 (1942).

57 "Principles and Aims of the American Birth Control League," appendix to *Margaret Sanger, The Pivot of Civilization* (New York: Brentano's, 1922), 277, in Roberts, *Killing the Black Body*, 75.

57 Ellen Chesler, *Woman of Valor: Margaret Sanger and the Birth Control Movement in America* (New York: Simon & Schuster, 1992), 216.

59 Letter to Margaret Sanger from unidentified client, March 11, 1936, Esther Katz, ed., *The Selected Papers of Margaret Sanger, Vol 2: Birth Control Comes of Age, 1928–1939* (Chicago: University of Illinois Press, 2006), 360.

60 Mary Ware Dennett to Carleton Dennett, January 10, 1915, folder 13, box 1, MWD Papers, in Chen, *The Sex Side of Life*, 172.

60–61 Mary Ware Dennett, *Who's Obscene?* (New York: Vanguard, 1930), 4, in Chen, *The Sex Side of Life*, 294.

61 "Mrs. Dennett's Fate to Be Decided Today; Author of Sex Pamphlet Says She Will Go to Jail Rather Than Pay Fine," *New York Times*, April 25, 1929, 6, http://timesmachine.nytimes.com/timesmachine/1929/04/25/95932599.html?pageNumber = 6.

61 *United States. v. Dennett*, 39 F.2d. 564, 569 (2d Cir. 1930).

61 *Youngs Rubber Corporation, Inc. v. C. I. Lee & Co.*, 45 F.2d 103, 107 (2d Cir. 1930).

61–62 Tone, *Devices and Desires*, 178.

62 *United States v. One Package*, 86 F.2d 737, 739 (2d Cir. 1936).

62 Ibid.

62 "Mrs. Sanger Gets Town Hall Medal; Birth Control Leader Praises U.S. Court for Ruling Liberalizing Law," *New York Times*, January 16, 1937, 16, http://timesmachine.nytimes.com/timesmachine/1937/01/16/94321406.html?pageNumber = 15.

62 Ibid.

63 Tone, *Devices and Desires*, 159.

65 Rickie Solinger, *Pregnancy and Power: A Short History of Reproductive Politics in America* (New York: New York University Press, 2005), 160.

65 Ibid.

66 Solinger, *Pregnancy and Power*, 149.

66 Ibid., 150.

66 Ibid., 151.

68 Tone, *Devices and Desires*, 208.

73 "Primary Sources: Correspondence between Pincus and Searle, Letter from Albert L. Raymond to Dr. Gregory Pincus," Pincus Papers, container 109, Library of Congress, Manuscripts

Division, October 4, 1957, in *The Pill, American Experience, PBS*, accessed July 12, 2013, http://www.pbs.org/wgbh/amex/pill/filmmore/ps_pincus.html.

73 Mrs. Jack Feit to Pincus, April 24, 1962, container 52, Pincus Papers, Manuscripts Division, Library of Congress, in Tone, *Devices and Desires*, 234.

74 Gloria Steinem, "The Moral Disarmament of Betty Coed," *Esquire*, September 1962, 155.

74–75 Ibid.,156.

75 Ibid., 157.

76 "The Pill: How It Is Affecting U.S. Morals, Family Life," *U.S. News & World Report*, July 11, 1966, in "Primary Sources: The Pill: Negatively Affecting U.S. Values?," *The Pill, American Experience, PBS*.

77 Tone, *Devices and Desires*, 254.

77 Dick Gregory, "My Answer to Genocide," *Ebony*, October 1971, 66, in Tone, *Devices and Desires*, 255.

78 *Griswold v. Connecticut*, 381 U.S. 479, 482.

78 Ibid., 484.

80 Dee Dee Bridgewater, "Draw the Line Storytelling," Center for Reproductive Rights, accessed March 15, 2015, http://www.drawtheline.org/stories/dee-dee-bridgewater-it-was-1968/.

81 Mohr, *Abortion in America*, 253.

82 Linda Greenhouse and Reva B. Siegel, *Before Roe v. Wade: Voices That Shaped the Abortion Debate before the Supreme Court's Ruling* (New Haven, CT: Yale Law School, 2012), ix, accessed March 5, 2015,http://documents.law.yale.edu/sites/default/files/BeforeRoe2ndEd_1.pdf.

82–83 Betty Friedan, "Abortion: A Woman's Civil Right," February 1969, in Greenhouse and Siegel, *Before Roe v. Wade*, 84.

83 Greenhouse and Siegel, *Before Roe v. Wade*, 280.

83 George Dugan, "State's & Catholic Bishops Ask Fight on Abortion Bill: Pastoral Letter Read," *New York Times*, February 13, 1967, 1, in Greenhouse and Siegel, *Before Roe v. Wade*, 282.

83 Judiciary Committee of the New Jersey Assembly, pamphlet submitted by New Jersey Catholic Conference, April 9, 1970, in Greenhouse and Siegel, *Before Roe v. Wade*, 84.

84 Dennis J. Horan et al, "The Case for the Unborn Child," *Abortion and Social Justice*, 1972, in Greenhouse and Siegel, *Before Roe v. Wade*, 89.

84 Judiciary Committee of the New Jersey Assembly, Public Testimony, April 9, 1970, in Greenhouse and Siegel, *Before Roe v. Wade*, 98.

85 "Women's Libbers Do Not Speak for Us," *The Phyllis Schlafly Report*, February 1972, in Greenhouse and Siegel, *Before Roe v. Wade*, 219.

86 Texas abortion law, quoted in Sarah Weddington, *A Question of Choice* (New York: Feminist Press, City University of New York, 2013), 42.

88 *Roe v. Wade*, 410 U.S. 113 (1973), 153.

89 Weddington, *A Question*, 164.

90 Anne, "Draw the Line Storytelling," Center for Reproductive Rights, accessed March 28, 2015, http://www .drawtheline.org/stories/very -wanted-child/.

90 Solinger, *Pregnancy and Power*, 205.

91 "Republican Party Political Platform of 1980," July 15, 1980, The American Presidency Project, accessed March 30, 2015, http:// www.presidency.ucsb.edu/ws /index.php?pid=25844.

91–92 "Democratic Party Political Platform of 1980," August 11, 1980, The American Presidency Project, accessed March 30, 2015, http://www.presidency.ucsb.edu/ ws/index.php?pid=29607.

93 *Planned Parenthood v. Casey*, 505 U.S. 833 (1992), 874.

93 Ibid., 877.

100 Nancy Stanwood, "Public Health in the Shadow of the First Amendment," YouTube video, 11:39, posted by "PRCHvideos," October 24, 2014, https://www .youtube.com/watch?v=mKf _HjeT_bs.

100 Pam Belluck, "Complex Science at Issue in Politics of Fetal Pain," *New York Times*, September 17, 2013, A1, A3.

101 Pain-Capable Unborn Child Protection Act, H.R. 36, section 2. (11), May 14, 2015, https://www .govtrack.us/congress/bills/114 /hr36/text.

105 Katrina Trinko, "Will Mississippi's Last Abortion Clinic Close?" *National Review* Online, December 18, 2012, http://www .nationalreview.com/article/ 335814/will-mississippis-last -abortion-clinic-close-katrina -trinko, in Rachel Benson Gold and Elizabeth Nash, "TRAP Laws Gain Political Traction While Abortion Clinics—and the Women They Serve—Pay the Price," *Guttmacher Policy Review* 16, no. 2 (Spring 2013), https://www .guttmacher.org/pubs/gpr/16/2 /gpr160207.html.

105 Arizona Senate Bill 1318, amending Arizona Revised Statutes, section 3, section 36-2153, A. 2. (h), March 11, 2015, http://www.azleg.gov/ legtext/52leg/1r/adopted/h.1318 -fsr.doc.htm.

105 Rick Rojas, "Arizona Orders Doctors to Say Abortions with Drugs May Be Reversible," *New York Times*, March 31, 2015, http://www.nytimes.com/2015/04/01/us/politics/arizona-doctors-must-say-that-abortions-with-drugs-may-be-reversed.html?ref=topics&_r=0.

107 Pope John Paul II, *Evangelium Vitae*, March 25, 1995, http://w2.vatican.va/content/john-paul-ii/en/encyclicals/documents/hf_jp-ii_enc_25031995_evangelium-vitae.html (August 9, 2015).

110 Rebecca Riffkin, "Fewest Americans Satisfied with Abortion Policies since 2001," Gallop, February 9, 2015, http://www.gallup.com/poll/181502/fewest-americans-satisfied-abortion-policies-2001.aspx?utm_source=abortion&utm_medium=search&utm_campaign=tiles.

110 Lydia Saad, "U.S. Still Split on Abortion: 47% Pro-Choice, 46% Pro-Life," Gallup, May 22, 2014, http://www.gallup.com/poll/170249/split-abortion-pro-choice-prolife.aspx?utm_source=abortion&utm_medium=search&utm_campaign=tiles.

112 Dr. Willie Parker, interview with the author, April 18, 2015.

112 Ibid.

112 Ibid.

115 Helen M. Alvaré, interview with the author, May 19, 2015.

115–116 Stephanie Toti, interview with the author, March 6, 2015.

116 "Abortion Access," Physicians for Reproductive Health, accessed May 15, 2015, http://prh.org/abortion/.

117 Stanwood, "Public Health in the Shadow."

119 Ruth Rosen, "Why the Relentless Assault on Abortion in the United States?," *History News Network*, George Mason University, July 29, 2013, http://historynewsnetwork.org/article/152758#.Ufvl7Ul0s98.email.

120 Michael Ollove, "States Aren't Eager to Regulate Fertility Industry," *USA Today*, March 19, 2015, in Center for Genetics and Society, http://www.geneticsandsociety.org/article.php?id=8457&&printsafe=1.

128 *Reproductive Rights Are Human Rights* (New York: Center for Reproductive Rights, 2009), 5, accessed July 29, 2014, http://reproductiverights.org/sites/crr.civicactions.net/files/documents/RRareHR_final.pdf.

130 Nancy Williamson, *Motherhood in Childhood: Facing the Challenge of Adolescent Pregnancy* (New York: United Nations Population Fund, 2013), v, accessed July 29, 2014, http://www.unfpa.org/publications/state-world-population-2013.

131 "New UN Report: Maternal Deaths Nearly Halved in 20 Years," World Health Organization, May 6, 2012, http://www.who.int/pmnch/media/news/2012/20120516_unfpa_report/en/.

131 Mahmoud F. Fathalla, "Human Rights Aspects of Safe Motherhood," *Best Practice and Research: Clinical Obstetrics & Gynecology* 20, no. 3 (June 2006): 409, in Nicholas D. Kristof and Sheryl WuDunn, *Half the Sky: Turning Oppression into Opportunity for Women Worldwide* (New York: Vintage, 2010), 116.

132 Kristof and WuDunn, *Half the Sky*, 117.

132 "New UN Report," World Health Organization.

135 "Preventing Unsafe Abortion," Media Center, Fact Sheet No. 388, World Health Organization, March 2014, http://who.int//mediacentre/factsheets/fs388/en/.

SELECTED BIBLIOGRAPHY

Alvaré, Helen M., professor of family law, George Mason University School of Law. Interview with the author, May 19, 2015.

Brodie, Janet Farrell. *Contraception and Abortion in 19th-Century America.* Ithaca, NY: Cornell University Press, 1994.

Center for Genetics and Society. Accessed June 2015. http://www .geneticsandsociety.org/index.php.

Center for Reproductive Rights. Accessed March 2015. http://www .reproductiverights.org/about-us.

Chen, Constance M. *"The Sex Side of Life": Mary Ware Dennett's Pioneering Battle for Birth Control and Sex Education.* New York: New Press, 1996.

Chesler, Ellen. *Woman of Valor: Margaret Sanger and the Birth Control Movement in America.* New York: Simon & Schuster, 1992.

D'Emilio, John, and Estelle B. Freedman. *Intimate Matters: A History of Sexuality in America*, 3rd ed. Chicago: University of Chicago Press, 2012.

Gordon, Linda. *Woman's Body, Woman's Right: A Social History of Birth Control in America.* New York: Viking, 1976.

Greenhouse, Linda, and Reva B. Siegel. *Before Roe v. Wade; Voices That Shaped the Abortion Debate before the Supreme Court Ruling.* New Haven, CT: Yale Law School, 2012. Accessed March 5, 2015. http://documents .law.yale.edu/sites/default/files/BeforeRoe2ndEd_1.pdf.

Guttmacher Institute. Accessed June 2015. http://www.guttmacher.org/.

Himes, Norman E. *Medical History of Contraception.* 1936. Reprint, New York: Schocken, 1970.

Kennedy, David M. *Birth Control in America: The Career of Margaret Sanger.* New Haven, CT: Yale University Press, 1970.

Kristof, Nicholas D., and Sheryl WuDunn. *Half the Sky: Turning Oppression into Opportunity for Women Worldwide.* New York: Vintage, 2010.

Margaret Sanger Papers Project. Accessed June 2014. http://www.nyu.edu /projects/sanger/.

Mohr, James C. *Abortion in America: The Origins and Evolution of National Policy, 1800–1900.* New York: Oxford University Press, 1978.

New York Society for the Suppression of Vice Records, Manuscript Division, Library of Congress, 1871–1953. Microfilm reel 2, 1986.

Norton, Mary Beth. *Liberty's Daughters: The Revolutionary Experience of American Women, 1750–1800.* Ithaca, NY: Cornell University Press, 1980.

Parker, Dr. Willie, abortion provider. Interview with the author, April 18, 2015.

Reproductive Rights Law: Where Is the Woman? Conference, Carr Center for Reproductive Justice, New York University School of Law, April 1, 2014. http://www.law.nyu.edu/centers/reproductivejustice/annualconference.

Riddle, John M. *Contraception and Abortion from the Ancient World to the Renaissance.* Cambridge, MA: Harvard University Press, 1992.

Riffkin, Rebecca. "Fewest Americans Satisfied with Abortion Policies since 2001." Gallup, February 9, 2015. http://www.gallup.com/poll/181502 /fewest-americans-satisfied-abortion-policies-2001.aspx?utm_source =abortion&utm_medium=search&utm_campaign=tiles.

Roberts, Dorothy. *Killing the Black Body: Race, Reproduction, and the Meaning of Liberty.* New York: Vintage, 1998.

Saad, Lydia. "Majority of Americans Still Support Roe v. Wade Decision." Gallup, January 22, 2013. http://www.gallup.com/poll/160058/majority -americans-support-roe-wade-decision.aspx?utm_source=abortion&utm_ medium=search&utm_campaign=tiles.

———. "US Still Split on Abortion: 47% Pro-Choice, 46% Pro-Life." Gallup, May 22, 2014. http://www.gallup.com/poll/170249/split-abortion-pro -choice-pro-life.aspx?utm_source=abortion&utm_medium=search&utm_ campaign=tiles.

Sanger, Margaret. *The Autobiography of Margaret Sanger.* Originally published as *Margaret Sanger: An Autobiography.* 1938. Reprint, New York: Dover Publications, 1971.

Solinger, Rickie. *Pregnancy and Power: A Short History of Reproductive Politics in America.* New York: New York University Press, 2005.

Tone, Andrea. *Devices and Desires: A History of Contraceptives in America.* New York: Farrar, Straus and Giroux, 2002.

Toti, Stephanie, senior counsel, Center for Reproductive Rights. Interview with the author, March 6, 2015.

Weddington, Sarah. *A Question of Choice.* New York: Feminist Press, City University of New York, 2013.

Williamson, Nancy. *Motherhood in Childhood; Facing the Challenge of Adolescent Pregnancy.* New York: United Nations Population Fund Publication, 2013. Accessed June 2015. http://www.unfpa.org /publications/state-world-population-2013.

Books

Archer, Jules. *The Feminist Revolution, a Story of the Three Most Inspiring and Empowering Women in American History: Susan B. Anthony, Margaret Sanger, and Betty Friedan*. New York: Sky Pony, 2015.

Friedman, Lauri S. *Teen Sex*. Farmington Hills, MI: Greenhaven, 2012.

Gerdes, Louise. *Human Genetics*. Farmington Hills, MI: Greenhaven, 2014.

Higgins, Nadia Abushanab. *Feminism: Reinventing the F-Word*. Minneapolis: Twenty-First Century Books, 2016.

Merino, Noel. *Abortion*. Farmington Hills, MI: Greenhaven, 2014.

Solinger, Rickie. *Reproductive Politics: What Everyone Needs to Know*. New York: Oxford University Press, 2013.

Steinem, Gloria. *My Life on the Road*. New York: Random House, 2015.

Websites

Advancing New Standards in Reproductive Health (ANSRH)
http://www.ansirh.org/about/mission.php.
ANSRH provides global social science research on and analysis of reproductive health issues.

Americans United for Life (AUL)
http://www.aul.org/about-aul/
AUL is an organization that promotes pro-life positions and distributes model legislation that states can use to draft their own antiabortion laws.

Mary Ware Dennett Papers
http://oasis.lib.harvard.edu/oasis/deliver/ ~ sch00058
The Schlesinger Library at Radcliffe College in Cambridge, Massachusetts, contains many of Dennett's papers and correspondence related to her work in the birth control and sex education movements.

NARAL Pro-Choice America
http://www.prochoiceamerica.org
NARAL advocates for and provides educational material on pro-choice issues.

National Right to Life Committee (NRLC)
http://www.nrlc.org/
NRLC educates the public about pro-life positions.

Planned Parenthood of America (PPA)
http://www.plannedparenthood.org/educators/resources/research-papers
PPA offers detailed information for teens and parents about reproductive and sexual health. The website also provides tools for educators in developing sex education programs.

Public Discourse
>
> http://www.thepublicdiscourse.com/author/helen-alvare/
> *Public Discourse* is an online journal of the Witherspoon Institute, which seeks to educate the public about the moral underpinnings of social issues. The website published articles by Helen Alvaré, a professor at George Mason University School of Law and pro-life supporter.

Sexuality Information and Education Council of the United States (SIECUS)
>
> http://siecus.org/
> SIECUS publishes many resources for educators, parents, and the public, including the *SIECUS Report*, a leading publication on sexuality issues.

World Health Organization
>
> http://www.who.int/en/
> Research and statistical data and analyses are provided on maternal, sexual, and reproductive health worldwide at this website.

Films and Interviews

Nancy Northrup, Executive Director of the Center for Reproductive Rights
>
> http://www.americanprogress.org/issues/women/news/2013/01/22/50176 /roe-at-40-podcast-series-interview-with-nancy-northup/. Podcast and written transcript of interview by Jessica Arons, director of the Women's Health and Rights Program at the Center for American Progress, January 22, 2013, 15:52. Northrup discusses the impact of *Planned Parenthood v. Casey* on reproductive rights.

Lynn Paltrow, Executive Director of the National Advocates for Pregnant Women
>
> https://www.americanprogress.org/issues/women/news/2013/06/21/67423 /interview-with-lynn-paltrow/. Podcast and written transcript of interview by Jessica Arons, director of the Women's Health and Rights Program at the Center for American Progress, June 21, 2013, 10:22. Paltrow discusses how fetal personhood laws restrict the rights of pregnant women.

The Pill
>
> This 2003 one-hour documentary, produced and directed by Chana Gazit for the American Experience (PBS), examines the history, development, and societal effect of the first birth control pill. The companion PBS website (www.pbs.org/wgbh/amex/pill/filmmore/) includes educational resources.

Dr. Nancy Stanwood, Physicians for Reproductive Health Board Chair and Associate Professor of Obstetrics and Gynecology, Yale University
>
> https://www.youtube.com/watch?v=mKf_HjeT_bs
> Panel discussion on "Public Health in the Shadow of the First Amendment," Yale Law School, January 18, 2014, 11:39. Stanwood discusses the issues facing abortion providers and their patients.

Charmaine Yoest, President of AUL, and Nancy Keenan, President of NARAL
>
> https://www.youtube.com/watch?v=iohPgyPK0WE
> PBS *NewsHour* interview by Gwen Ifill, "The Debate on Abortion, Four Decades after *Roe vs. Wade*," January 22, 2013, 9:47. Yoest and Keenan discuss abortion forty years after *Roe*.

PHOTO ACKNOWLEDGMENTS

ABOUT THE AUTHOR

Vicki Oransky Wittenstein has always been curious about new ideas, people, and places. That curiosity has taken her life in many directions. So far, she has been a student, a criminal prosecutor, a writer, and an advocate for children and families. She is the author of a number of science and history articles for young readers, as well as the middle-grade title *Planet Hunter: Geoff Marcy and the Search for Other Earths*, winner of the 2011 Science Communication Award from the American Institute of Physics (AIP), and the YA title *For the Good of Mankind? The Shameful History of Human Medical Experimentation*, a Junior Library Guild selection. She and her husband live in Brooklyn, New York, and have two children. You can learn more about her at www.vickiwittenstein.com.